This book gave me a deep sense of assurance and encouragement that leading for impact beyond the immediate business focus is not a side task. It's at the heart of proactive leadership. Stephen and Bronwyn are trusted voices in the shift from compliance to leadership grounded in impact and resilience.

So many dimensions are explored here. It's a reference leaders will return to and want to share.

—Bernie Kelly
Mentor: Fit FOR PURPOSE Leaners and Organisations;
Co-Author: For Purpose Leaders Navigating What Matters

Bronwyn Reid and Dr Stephen Morse take what can feel like an overwhelming, jargon-heavy concept and translate it into a practical, inspiring roadmap for SMEs. This is not just a business book - it's a call to action for every SME leader who wants to contribute to a more sustainable, equitable economy and thrive in the process.

—Mark Jones
Co-founder and Chief Storyteller, Impact Institute

Reid and Morse strip away jargon, offering clear, real-world strategies that prove small enterprises can lead meaningful change. I especially valued the case studies on modern slavery, inclusive hiring, and cyber resilience — topics often overlooked in SME discussions. Warm, clear, and motivating, this book turns ESG from an abstract concept into a practical roadmap for doing good and doing well.

Talita Meira, CEO of Luksai, Doctor of Business Administration Candidate, Visiting Scholar – Goizueta Business School, Emory University

—Talita Meira
CEO of Luksai, Doctor of Business Administration Candidate,
Visiting Scholar – Goizueta Business School, Emory University

SMALL
BUSINESS

BIG
IMPACT

Why ESG won't save you
but Smart Strategy &
Real Action will

BRONWYN REID &
DR STEPHEN MORSE

First Published 2025

Published by Bronwyn Reid & Dr Stephen Morse

Produced by Indie Experts
www.indieexpertspublishing.com

Cover design and typesetting by
Ammie Christiansen, Fast Forward Design
Typeset in 12pt Adobe Garamond Pro

Cataloguing-in-Publication data is available from the
National Library of Australia

ISBN:
978-1-7642486-2-4 (Printed)
978-1-7642486-1-7 (eBook)

Disclaimer:
Any information in the book is purely the opinion of the author
based on her personal experience and should not be taken as
business or legal advice. All material is provided for educational
purposes only. We recommend to always seek the advice of a
qualified professional before making any decision regarding
personal and business needs.

Foreword

Welcome to a well written and candid assessment of both the obligations and expectations that all Australian business owners and managers must consider. Some who've been in business a while will find this a fresh perspective on how the concept of corporate responsibility has "moved on". For start-up and SME's businesses looking to create sustainable businesses - this is a must read as they look to craft a compelling business strategy.

The concept that every business must make an effort to contribute to a more caring economy is real (and to some degree legislated). But in addition to that today's consumers want small business to make that effort and are more likely to reward businesses and brands that care (or at least are trying to care) with their loyalty. Gen Z consumers are making financial decisions on the basis now and Gen Alpha will be very soon.

The "R" word in terms of how SME business owners view risk and how effectively they can report data to prove compliance has significant, potentially positive, consequences that may actually make them a more sustainable and potentially valuable business.

Small Business Big Impact is a comprehensive "primer" for SME business owners. It raises the important issues from a statutory compliance perspective but also shows how it can be applied to engage staff and inform customers on the positive actions being taken. The direction provided can help create better businesses.

The most recent research identifies the City of Sydney being home to approximately 24,000 businesses*. Among these is the largest number and diversity of SMEs in Australia, and we look forward to leveraging the thinking outlined here to help them make a a bigger ESG impact.

Peter May | Executive Officer, *CBD Sydney Chamber of Commerce*

*2023 City of Sydney Business Needs Survey prepared by Oxford Economics Australia

Contents

Introduction

In *Small Business, Big Impact* authors Bronwyn Reid and Dr Stephen Morse dissect and explain the contribution small business makes to the wider world through the lens of ESG and (their special ingredient) 'R' for reporting.

I must admit I thought I knew about the Environmental, Social and Governance movement but this book takes things to a whole new level.

Here is a concept that in its current form is barely 20 years old. It emerged out of the Corporate, Social, Responsibility (or CSR) movement in response, I think, to the need to ensure that business wasn't just run profitably but also ethically.

I am sure there have been many drivers behind the rise of the CSR then the ESG then the ESGR movements however it surely wasn't a coincidence that this kind of thinking should emerge in an era of peace and prosperity underpinned by globalisation.

Businesses both big and small understand that longevity cannot be achieved without social licence, without the support of the community, without respecting the environment and basic human rights of those engaged in the workplace and in the supply chain.

The point, I think, of this book is that business can be about both profit and doing the right thing. What a simple but effective concept!

I am especially impressed by the way the authors lay out their case and cite business examples to illustrate their point.

This isn't a book of thoughts and ideas, it's an ideas-based manual for achieving better outcomes for business and the community! Indeed, there's no shortage of books about big business but this book—*Small Business, Big Impact*—though aimed at small business has lessons for us all.

Here is a book where statements are supported by evidence. Here is a book that will make a difference to business owners, to businesses, and to their communities.

Bernard Salt AM

Preface

We humans are weird creatures. We come up with an idea, a way of thinking—Richard Dawkins would call it a "meme"—and hold on to it ferociously. Until we don't.

Not that changing our collective mind is a bad thing. In fact, in most cases it's a good move. Imagine if we all still thought that left-handedness is a sign of evil or weakness? Or you could tell if someone was a witch by dunking them in water?

The point is that beliefs change over time. Often, there is a long lag between when someone pops their head above the parapets and says, "I think that's wrong", and when we all get to "How did we ever believe that?" Mostly the new, improved version sticks around for a while until another change sweeps through.[1]

This book is about one of those changes. It's taken quite a long time to emerge from the obscurity of academic papers and the fringe press, but it's here now, and we must get on the change train or be left behind.

It's about why and how businesses operate. Do they just look after their shareholders, or do they work to make the world a better place?

Inevitably, there are some acronyms, and this book is centred on one of them: ESG. It stands for Environmental, Social, and Governance. If you add "Responsibilities" or "Reporting" to the end, it makes more sense. This book covers the things you must do to meet your environmental, social and governance responsibilities as a business owner or manager.

This book explains the history of ESG—how, why and where it emerged. For now, know that it's had a stop-start journey to where we are now. But for some, it's a new concept and, understandably, can seem quite daunting or just another thing to do and another cost to bear. Big organisations have teams of people to think about and deal with this stuff. As an SME owner or manager, you most probably don't.

What we are trying to create with this book is a framework that SME owners and managers can use to start their ESG evolution without the overwhelm. We want to stop them disengaging before they get started because it's all just too hard.

Our hope is that this book will help you to understand ESG, where it came from, why it's a good thing, and how you can start implementing your own changes.

Chapter 1
What Do the E, the S and the G Stand for?

First, the acronyms.

Collectively, "ESG" is how we measure the performance of an organisation beyond its simple financial achievements. We have been measuring financial performance for centuries.[2] We now measure other critical aspects of business operations as well, such as environmental impact, social responsibility, and governance practices.

E = Environmental

S = Social

G = Governance

It's a rather awkward acronym. The three letters stand for two adjectives and a noun. It needs another letter at the end to describe what is really meant. An "R" would be good—R for Reporting, or Responsibilities. Both those words imply action, that you must do something—either report on something or be responsible for something.

However, the term ESG is well entrenched now, so it's no use trying to change its use. But keep that silent "R" in mind as a reminder that ESG is something you have to *do*, not just a random concept that somebody thought up.

And another acronym…

To explain ESG, we must deal with yet another acronym: CSR, which stands for Corporate Social Responsibility. Oh no, says the small business owner or manager. More letters for me to learn.

The Evolution of ESG

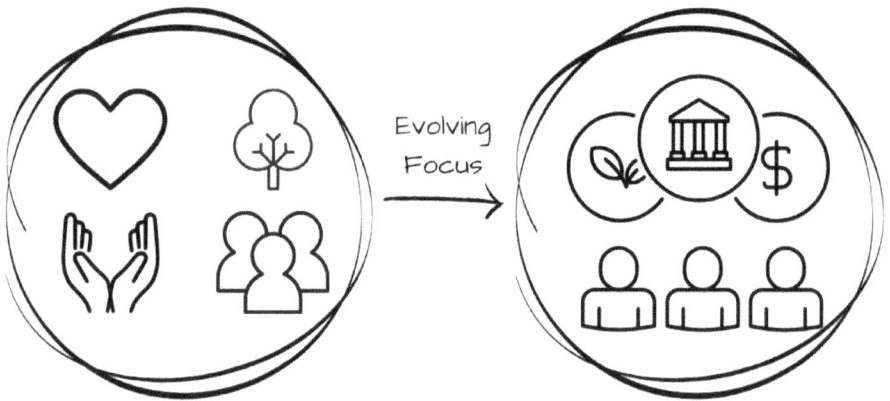

Evolving Focus

CSR

Corporate Social Responsibility

Broad, Voluntary,
Not Measured

ESG(R)

Environmental, Social, Governance

Measurable, Reported,
Embedded in Company Operations

*Don't forget the R -
for Responsibilities and Reporting

CSR is a broad term. (That's the problem with social science concepts. They don't have nice, neat definitions like maths, physics and chemistry.) CSR is a company's obligation and commitment to be a positive force in society. It involves voluntary initiatives that extend beyond legal obligations, such as philanthropic efforts, community engagement, and environmental conservation projects. CSR emphasises a company's moral obligation to "give back" and is typically viewed as an extension of a business's brand and public image. Unlike financial performance, CSR does not have standardised metrics for assessment.

CSR is a company's obligation and commitment to be a positive force in society.

ESG arose after, and out of, CSR. ESG is a more structured, data-driven framework used by investors, regulators, and stakeholders to measure a company's sustainability and ethical performance. It focuses on specific measurable criteria across three pillars: Environmental (e.g., carbon emissions, energy efficiency), Social (e.g., labour practices, diversity), and Governance (e.g., board structure, executive compensation, decision-making guidelines). Because they do affect long-term financial performance and risk management, ESG allows them to be brought into core business operations, investment decision-making and corporate strategies. Unlike CSR, ESG has become deeply embedded in financial markets, with standardized reporting metrics and global frameworks. It is these ESG frameworks that we hope to make accessible to SME owners and managers like you. We want you to understand:

- What this is all about
- Why it's a good thing
- Why you need to do it
- How you can go about it simply.

The E – Environmental

The E is the easiest of the three letters to deal with. To a greater or lesser degree, we all know what environmental responsibility and environmental awareness are and what we should aspire to. We know that we should not throw our rubbish in the river or drop it on the ground. We know we should recycle our bottles and cans.

But here's the thing. We don't always stop to think about the full impact of our actions. We recycle when it's easy, avoid plastic when we remember, and generally try to do the right thing. But how often do we pause to consider what happens behind the scenes? What's involved in producing, packaging, and transporting all the stuff we consume?

The Ripple Effect of Littering

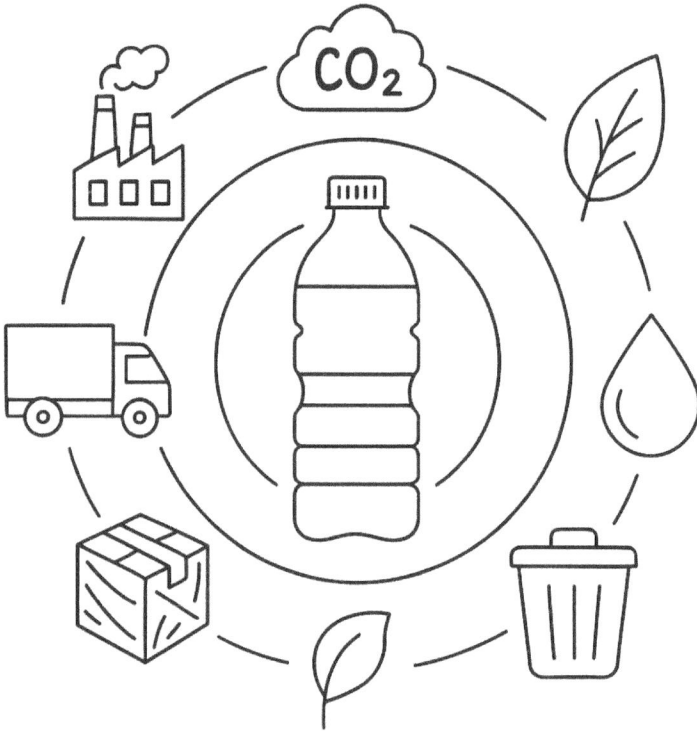

I (Bronwyn) chaired a discussion panel at a conference in Singapore for the mass participation sports industry, an industry I know little about. The panel addressed the environmental impact of mass participation sports—events such as the Boston Marathon, the London Marathon or the City2Surf Marathon in Sydney. Those events are accompanied by copious amounts of merchandise. Every participant gets something: a T-shirt, a water bottle, a souvenir pen…

Every single one of those T -shirts is wrapped in plastic, then 10 of them are wrapped in plastic, then 10 bundles of 10 are wrapped in plastic, then 100 bundles of 10 are wrapped in plastic and put on a pallet. And then the pallet is wrapped in plastic. And all this plastic goes to landfill the moment the marathon is over. But there's a lot more to the environment than just plastic and bottles on the ground. It encompasses our use of renewable energy, reducing our carbon footprint, the quantity of fossil fuels we are using. My environmental company runs a fleet of diesel vehicles. We're acutely aware of it.

It's about efficiency in our use of natural resources. I just mentioned my company's fleet of diesel vehicles. They are all kept fully serviced and fully maintained. That's our way of trying to make sure that we're being as efficient as we can in the use of those diesel vehicles.

It's about efficiency in our use of energy. If we change to using LED light bulbs and or turn off the lights, computers, and TVs at night, we will be more efficient in our energy use.

It's about efficiency in our use of water. Are the kids standing under the shower for 25 minutes every night? Do we have drought-tolerant plants in our gardens?

Our environmental awareness, and therefore our responsibilities, change over time. We all generate waste in our businesses, so let's look beyond the simple concept of not dropping our rubbish on the ground. In the end, it comes down to efficiency—being mindful about how we use what we've got, and making smarter choices wherever we can. We talk about the 5 Rs in waste management.

- **Reduce.** Just don't use as much. How much do you actually have to use?

- **Repair.** I don't know if anyone reading this is old enough to remember repairing your clothes. It's certainly a rare event now. Back then, you would take your vacuum cleaner to the electrical store and the person at the electrical store would repair it. Not now. We just throw things away and go to Harvey Norman and get a new one.

- **Repurpose.** I have a friend, Jane Milburn, who specialises in what she calls "upcycling". She takes clothes, some of which by her own admission are pretty daggy and not on the high end of fashion. Jane repurposes them into high-fashion garments.

- **Rot.** A responsible way to dispose of organic waste is to let it rot instead of just sending it to landfill, where it sits. A covered landfill is an anaerobic environment, an environment without oxygen. Organic waste stays there for a very long time. A head of lettuce will take up to 25 years to decompose in anaerobic conditions. We can imagine an archaeologist, some 3,000 years from now, digging up the landfill and wondering what it was that we were feeding ourselves!

- **Recycle.** Recycling is not an easy topic. It's a big topic and it's a big rabbit hole we could go down, but that's not for this book. I hope that we are all making some attempt to recycle.

The S – Social

Your business does not exist in isolation, in a vacuum separated from the remainder of society. There are entry points and exit points between you, your business, and your local community, society, and the economy as a whole. Our social responsibility is how we interact with the wider world. That responsibility begins within our own four walls, with how we treat our employees, and extends outward from there.

Fair Pay

At a bare minimum, "social" encompass things like paying people who work at our companies correctly. That sounds incredibly basic, but there are recurring news items that tell us it is a real problem. We hear about companies being fined for failing to pay their workers correctly. And these are just the cases that make it into the public eye. Many more likely go unnoticed or unreported.[3]

Discrimination, Harassment and Bullying

Legally, harassment, bullying, and discrimination in the workplace are not allowed— certainly in most developed nations, and in many developing nations as well. There is also an international framework that addresses this issue.

In 2019, the International Labour Organization (ILO) adopted Convention No. 190. This was the first international treaty recognizing the right to a workplace free from violence and harassment, including gender-based harassment. Countries ratifying this convention commit to implementing measures to prevent and address workplace harassment.

But practically, it still happens. Every. Single. Day.

Working Conditions

The work conditions you provide for employees... Are they clean? Are they healthy? Are they damaging hearing? Are they sanitary?

Like our environmental obligations, social obligations are not static. 4T Consultants can provide some cogent examples. What we are noticing in our environmental company's work is the increasing frequency and intensity of storms. Hence, we are cognizant about the safety of our workers in the field with hazards such as lightning strikes. We also now have temperature cut-off points, where field teams are withdrawn from outdoor work. When we started the business almost 30 years ago, encountering those extremes was a relatively rare event. Now, we can experience days (or weeks) on end of extreme heat.

Local impact

Supporting your local community takes many forms, both as an individual and as a business leader. On a personal level, it might mean helping the Parents and Citizens Association at the local school, volunteering as a referee for football or netball games, selling tickets for the annual school concert, or contributing to any of the countless small acts that help our communities thrive. From a business perspective, it's about fostering a culture where your team is encouraged and supported to actively participate in community initiatives, strengthening connections and shared purpose.

Modern Slavery

You might think, "This doesn't apply to me living in Australia", but that's not the case. Australia has specific legislation addressing modern slavery. Under the Modern Slavery Act 2018, all companies with an annual turnover of more than $100 million are required to report on their efforts to identify and address modern slavery risks within their supply chains. This includes investigating whether products they source are manufactured in factories overseas where workers face conditions akin to slavery.

Modern slavery is also a significant issue within Australia itself. The agriculture sector, for instance, has faced scrutiny for exploiting backpackers and foreign visa workers during harvest seasons. In some cases, these workers have endured conditions that, effectively, amount to modern slavery.

The G – Governance

Governance is how you run your business and how things get done. What are the rules in your place of work? What policies, procedures, and processes are used?

In the previous section, some pertinent social issues were discussed. Does your company have policies and procedures that cover them? I recall the first time I was asked whether our company had a Modern Slavery Policy whilst preparing a tender response. I had never even thought of such a thing. Do you have an occupational health and safety policy? Do you have a policy and a procedure for working in the heat?

Governance is also about risk management. If your business is impacted by a harmful event, many other people are impacted as well. In a family business it's you, and it's probably your spouse and your children, too. If you have a business partner, it's your partner, your partner's partner, and their children. Then there are your employees, your suppliers, and your customers. How are you organising your business to minimise those impacts? That is part of your governance responsibility.

Governance is about being ethical, transparent, and accountable. Unfortunately, we don't have to look too far to see the examples of bad governance, even in Australian companies.

Governance is simply about being ethical,
transparent, and accountable.
– Bronwyn Reid

A recent and well-known case of corporate governance failure is the Australian airline Qantas. The airline was knowingly selling tickets on flights that had already been cancelled. It is disquieting that someone in a senior position, maybe even at board level, thought something like: "Here's a good idea. We will extract money from our customers by not disclosing the truth. We'll invest the money for ourselves in the meantime until eventually we may give it back."

- Did anyone ask if that was ethical?
- Do you think what Qantas did was transparent?
- Did Qantas accept accountability for those decisions and actions? No—not until required to do so by the courts.

Another example from corporate Australia is the supermarket duopoly, Coles and Woolworths. Out of every $10 Australians spend on groceries, $6.50 goes to the big two. The competition is fierce, with both continually advertising reduced prices. Except the prices allegedly went up before they went down. At the time of writing, a class action lawsuit is under way alleging that the duo engaged in deceptive pricing by raising prices by at least 15% for a short time before announcing "discounts".[4]

Again, is that practice ethical? Is it transparent? Are they being accountable to their customers?

The dangers of greenwashing

Following that brief 40,000-foot flyover of the E and the S and the G, how are you feeling?

Frightened and overwhelmed? Ready to press on? A bit confident because you are "doing something"?

That brings us to the next question. Why can't a company advertise that it is being responsible and foresighted in its environmental, social, and governance actions? Surely the customers will see the advertising and promotion and buy their goods and services.

Unfortunately, it's not that easy. Many countries, Australia included, have corporate regulators to track "greenwashing". Greenwashing is the close relative of "whitewashing". Both involve using false information to portray a situation as better than it actually is. Greenwashing means using false information about "environmentally friendly" products, services or practices. Regulators are taking an increasingly hard line, issuing significant fines. So far, Volkswagen holds the record for the largest fine. Volkswagen's use of software to falsify data from vehicle emissions tests cost the company $34.69 billion in fines and settlements.[5]

Several Australian companies have also been prosecuted and fined (but not nearly enough, in my opinion) for greenwashing. Beneath the façade of eco-friendly claims, their internal systems, policies and procedures often conceal activities that are far from environmentally sustainable.

Chapter 2
The History of ESG

At the outset of this book, we knew it was important to provide context—and to dispel the myth that ESG is a recent invention. What we didn't expect was how deep and fascinating the history would be. The path to where we are today is long and complex (worthy of its own book, perhaps), but we've aimed to give you a clear, high-level overview to help make sense of how we got here—and where we might be heading next. There are two ways to view the history of ESG: the short version, and the comprehensive version.

The short version.

The short version attributes the beginning of ESG to a 2004 United Nations Report, *Who Cares Wins: Connecting Financial Markets to a Changing World*.[6] Note the words "Financial Markets" in the subtitle. This explains why the term ESG is so often used as an abbreviation for ESG investing, which is the practice of choosing financial investments based upon a company's environmental impact, social responsibility, and governance practices. ESG investing is also referred to as ethical, sustainable, or responsible investing. In this book, though, we have taken a much broader definition of ESG, not just the investing bit.

The comprehensive version.

As we noted earlier, ESG arose out of Corporate Social Responsibility (CSR). CSR is a much broader term, encompassing a company's responsibilities beyond the purely financial. This wider definition highlights how the relationship between organisations and society has changed over time. The story of how we moved from shareholder profit to stakeholder impact starts a long time ago—with the creation of the modern company itself.

Origins of Joint-Stock Companies (1600s)

The modern company structure (joint-stock company) emerged in the 1600s, when colonial powers were venturing overseas for trade and exploration. That expansion was very risky and costly, so the joint-stock company was invented as a way for several people to pool their resources for these ventures. Companies such as the British East India Company and the Dutch East India Company allowed investors to share both the risks and the rewards.

Profits were not the only purpose, however. Governments required them to have a purpose apart from profits. In return for the limited liability, (which protected the shareholders' personal assets from being used to pay the company's debts or liabilities), the companies had to provide an explicit rationale for their establishment. The purpose stated would be something like the value and strategic benefit they would bring to the nation, the contribution they would make to national wealth, the establishment of new trade routes, the expansion of territories, and so on. From our modern vantage point, not all those purposes were acceptable because they included taking slaves, exploiting humans and natural resources, genocide… But we can detect the spark of CSR. Corporations had a responsibility to society apart from making profits.

Industrial Revolution and Exploitation Late 1700s—Mid-1800s

Once the joint-stock corporation had been invented, it proved to be incredibly successful.

The Industrial Revolution, which began in the late 1700s and continued through the 1800s, transformed economies from primarily agricultural to industrialised systems. It was a period of rapid growth in manufacturing, driven by mechanised production and a surge in demand for goods—especially along those newly expanded global trade routes.

Corporate power expanded significantly alongside industrial growth. As corporations grew, the concept of shareholder primacy began to dominate, asserting that a company's main responsibility was to maximize financial returns to its shareholders.

The downside of this rapid industrialization was harsh working conditions including long hours, low wages, and dangerous environments. Child labour was widespread. Worker protections were minimal, leading to frequent injuries and even deaths in workplaces.

Poor working conditions led to widespread poverty, and, for many, debt became a near-permanent condition. Debtors' prisons were common, as people could be incarcerated for failing to repay even minor debts, often falling further into poverty while incarcerated.

The Industrial Era and the Robber Barons (1800s–1900s)

As awareness of these injustices grew, reformers advocated for change. In Europe, social reformers, labour unions, and politicians began pushing for worker protections and child labour laws, eventually leading to the first labour regulations and safety standards in industries like mining and textiles.

In the United States, the late 1800s saw the emergence of wealthy and influential industrial magnates, including John D. Rockefeller, Andrew Carnegie, and J.P. Morgan. These individuals amassed vast fortunes and controlled significant sectors of the economy, such as oil, steel, and railroads, often through monopolistic practices.

These "robber barons" were notorious for prioritizing profits and consolidating power. They often crushed competition, influenced politics, and resisted labour reforms. In their drive for profits, they maintained poor working conditions and low wages for workers, who had little power and few legal protections.

Not surprisingly, this period saw significant labour unrest, with strikes and protests becoming common. Labour advocates, reformers, and even some business leaders argued for a model in which companies would also consider workers' welfare, public health, and the environment.

The unrest also worked to promote public awareness of labour rights, gradually leading to reforms. Once again, companies were required to look beyond profits and had to take social factors into account.

First steps toward responsibility: In response to public outrage and pressure at the excesses of the robber barons, some industrialists, notably Andrew Carnegie, began promoting philanthropy and social responsibility. Carnegie's book, *Gospel of Wealth*, argued that the rich had a duty to give back to society, leading him to donate much of his own wealth to public institutions.[7]

Corporate accountability begins: Corporations continued to grow in power, but the idea that businesses had a social obligation beyond profits also started to gain traction. However, these early CSR initiatives were often limited and did not yet form a comprehensive framework like modern ESG.

Impact on Australian Businesses

During this same period, Australia's economy was industrialising, with mining, agriculture, and manufacturing driving national growth. While Australia did not have direct "robber barons" like those in the United States, large corporations dominated key industries, often exploiting labourers, including Indigenous Australians and migrant workers.

- The Harvester Judgment (1907) in Australia was a landmark case that established the concept of a "fair and reasonable" minimum wage, a direct response to corporate exploitation.

- Early trade union movements fought for better working conditions, setting the stage for modern workplace regulations and ESG-aligned labour rights laws in Australia.

The Industrial Revolution and the era of the robber barons, therefore, represents a critical stage in the evolution of corporate accountability. It sparked reforms that would later shape stakeholder capitalism and the modern emphasis on ESG, balancing financial success with societal responsibility.

The Rise of Corporate Social Responsibility (CSR) (1930s–1980s)

The period from the 1930s to the 1980s was a tug-o-war between corporate social responsibility and the interests of companies and institutional investors.

The period kicked off with the Great Depression, a massive shock to government, companies, and society in general. Philanthropy was largely focused on elite causes, such as funding cultural institutions, universities, and museums. The rapid and brutal economic collapse of the Depression left a deep scar on society. Millions found themselves out of work almost overnight, with no safety nets to fall back on. Families were evicted, forced into makeshift shelters, and queued at soup kitchens just to survive. In the face of such widespread suffering, some companies began to rethink their role. They realised that looking after their employees wasn't just good ethics—it was essential for survival.

Productivity and loyalty couldn't be expected from people who were hungry, sick, or sleeping rough. Out of both compassion and necessity, some businesses initiated support programs to help their workers weather the storm. These efforts, born in a time of desperation, laid the groundwork for more formalised Corporate Social Responsibility practices in the decades that followed.

Collaboration with Government and Nonprofits

The scale of the Great Depression's challenges was far beyond what any single organization could address. In addition, many companies had been bankrupted or even taken over by the government[8] during the protracted downturn. Public–private partnerships emerged as companies, government agencies, and nonprofit organizations worked together to provide relief—a departure from their previously siloed roles. The cooperation lay the groundwork for modern CSR partnerships.

Distrust Rising

The Great Depression also brought rising distrust of corporate power and again sparked a debate about the role and purpose of corporations. Public sentiment began to shift again, and the mood was clear. Making money was no longer the only measure of success. Social contribution mattered too.

Influence of Labor Movements

The rise of labour movements and trade unions across Europe during and after the Great Depression played a significant role in shaping corporate practices. These movements demanded better wages, working conditions, and labour protections, pressuring companies to adopt more socially responsible policies. The influence of unions ensured that CSR in Europe became closely tied to workers' rights and social welfare.

The Rise of Stakeholder Capitalism: The aftermath of World War II

World War II caused more global business and societal fracture and created the circumstances for different approaches to capitalism in Europe and north America.

Both the United States and Europe faced the gargantuan task of rebuilding. Both entered a period of economic growth with a sense of optimism after the horrors of a long war, the so-called "Golden Age of Capitalism".

But their approaches to rebuilding and what we would now term CSR/ESG-related issues diverged, shaped by their distinct political, economic, and cultural contexts.

European countries adopted a more holistic approach to reconstruction and engaged all stakeholders in the recovery efforts, emphasizing cooperation between government, businesses, and labour unions. The sheer scale of devastation required coordinated national efforts to rebuild economies, infrastructure, and social systems. Strong welfare systems and an emphasis on stakeholder participation in decision-making became integral to the rebuild.

In contrast to Europe's stakeholder-driven approach, the United States pursued a shareholder capitalism model, prioritizing economic expansion and corporate independence over state-led coordination.

1950s–1960s Peak CSR?

As the post-WWII reconstruction accelerated, so did economic growth. In fact, the world economic growth rate for 1950–1973 was twice the rate of the previous 80 years.[9] This growth was seen as a demonstration of the power of capitalism vs the centrally planned economies of the Eastern Bloc.

The Cold War emerged after World War II as tensions rose between the United States and the Soviet Union over competing political ideologies. The Eastern Bloc referred to the group of Soviet-aligned socialist states in Eastern Europe.

The concept of corporate responsibility did not disappear, however. In 1953, American economist Howard R. Bowen wrote a book entitled *Social Responsibilities of the Businessman*, whose release ignited more discussion about corporate accountability. That book is considered to be the first comprehensive discussion of business ethics and social responsibility, and it drove broader debate about the role of businesses in society.

1960s social movements: Vietnam, Civil Rights, and Environmentalism

Then came the 1960s and huge societal change, particularly in the United States. The Civil Rights movement and anti-Vietnam war demonstrations raised public awareness of social injustices. What began as student protests evolved into wider political activism. Environmental issues also became topics of discussion. Rachael Carson published her influential book *Silent Spring* in 1962, raising awareness of the damage done to the environment by some chemicals. Communities wanted companies to take notice of them and take their needs into account.

The 1970s and the contest of ideas

The elevated expectations of corporate conduct that emerged from the 1960s clashed with growing globalisation and shareholder capitalism in the 1970s, and the fallout was to last for decades. In 1970, influential American economist Milton Friedman published a seminal paper, "The Social Responsibility of Business Is to Increase Its Profits".[10] He argued that a corporation's sole responsibility is to maximize profits. The idea took hold and dominated corporate governance agendas, sidelining broader social responsibilities for decades to come.

But an undercurrent of CSR positivity remained.

- In 1965, activist Ralph Nader published *Unsafe at Any Speed*, an investigation of the US automobile industry and its safety standards.[11] Nader advocated for companies to be subject to a charter that would set out their responsibilities and rights, taking company law right back to the 1600s! He was not successful.

- The Committee for Economic Development in the United States also published a report, "A New Rationale for Corporate Social Policy".[12] This quote from the foreword sums up the content: "To what extent can corporate involvement in social problem-solving be justified when such activity lies outside the usual framework of the marketplace?"

- The first Earth Day was held in April 1970 in the United States with the express purpose of pressuring governments into passing laws to protect the environment. It seems incredible now, but until then, there were no laws at all to prevent environmental pollution.[13]

1980s and 1990s: The battle of ideas continues

Environmental concerns dominated in the 1980s and 1990s. Human-induced climate change, the struggles of the Third World, pollution, and damage to the ozone layer were top of mind. International agencies stepped up and established forums to understand and deal with these issues.

- World Commission on Environment and Development[14]

- United Nations Environment Program (UNEP) Statement of Commitment by Financial Institutions on Sustainable Development[15]

- United Nations Conference on Environment and Development (Rio Earth Summit)[16]

- United Nations Framework Convention on Climate Change (UNFCCC), or what we now refer to as Conference of the Parties (COP)[17]

- Montreal Protocol on Substances that Deplete the Ozone Layer[18]

- Kyoto Protocol[19]

- Global Reporting Initiative 1997[20]

With all that activity and attention, CSR did begin taking root, especially in the United States and Europe. Some companies started to adopt practices beyond profit-making, including social and environmental programs. However, CSR in this era was regarded as voluntary and supplementary to the primary mission of profit maximization.

But Friedman was not consigned to irrelevance. The Friedman doctrine of shareholder primacy remained and grew, dominating corporate thinking right through the 1980s, 1990s and the early 2000s. Combined with the different approach to capitalism taken by the United States after World War II, the result has been flexible labour markets, corporate behaviour influenced by capital markets, and the prioritising of short-term financial gains over long-term, socially responsible practices—echoes of the "profits-over-people" mentality associated with the original robber baron era.

The 2000s: Crisis, Collapse, and the Birth of ESG

Just when it seemed that Friedman and his followers had won the ideas war, several corporate scandals and collapses pressed the Pause button. These effectively blew up international capital markets in the 2000s. The following list is by no means exhaustive.

- Enron
- WorldCom
- Long-Term Capital Management (1998)
- Arthur Andersen
- Parmalat

Australia made its contribution as well, with

- One.Tel
- HIH Insurance

These high-profile collapses revealed deep-seated governance failures, fraudulent financial practices, and reckless risk-taking.

Against this backdrop of economic and social upheaval, the conversation around corporate responsibility began to shift again. In the early 2000s, Corporate Social Responsibility (CSR) was still largely voluntary and driven by reputation management. But the sheer scale and impact of these corporate scandals, environmental disasters, and financial crises sparked a demand for something more robust and enforceable. The consequences of unchecked corporate behaviour became impossible to ignore.

The Rise of ESG as a Formal Framework

Out of these business crises, global organizations laid the foundations for ESG as a structured and measurable approach to corporate responsibility.

1. The UN Global Compact (2000)

   » The United Nations launched the Global Compact, urging companies to align with ten principles covering human rights, labour standards, environmental protection, and anti-corruption.

   » This was a major shift from voluntary CSR efforts to a more structured global initiative focused on corporate responsibility.

2. The Birth of ESG (2004–2006)

   » In 2004, former UN Secretary-General Kofi Annan called on financial institutions to consider environmental, social, and governance factors in investment decisions.

   » This led to the publication in 2004 of the landmark report "Who Cares Wins", which introduced the term ESG and linked responsible corporate behaviour to financial performance.

   » That same year, the UNEP Finance Initiative's Freshfields Report emphasized the legal justification for integrating ESG into investment decision-making.

   » In 2006, the Principles for Responsible Investment (PRI) was launched, providing institutional investors with a framework to consider ESG risks and opportunities when managing assets.

A Shift from CSR to ESG

These developments marked a fundamental shift from CSR as a "nice to have" public relations tool to ESG as a data-driven, risk-informed investment criterion. ESG wasn't just about doing good anymore; it was about managing risk, building resilience, and ensuring long-term value for both shareholders and society.

Environmental Disasters and the Push for Sustainability

While corporate governance scandals dominated the early 2000s, environmental responsibility also became a focal point after major ecological disasters.

- The BP Deepwater Horizon Oil Spill in 2010 was the largest environmental disaster in petroleum industry history. It exposed the devastating consequences of poor risk management and weak regulatory oversight.

- The growing climate crisis led to greater pressure on corporations to reduce emissions, with the Kyoto Protocol (1997) and subsequent climate summits pushing for stronger action.

- Companies began integrating sustainability into their business models, leading to the rise of the corporate sustainability movement.

This period saw the mainstream adoption of sustainability reporting, with organizations like the Global Reporting Initiative (GRI) and Dow Jones Sustainability Index (DJSI) offering benchmarks for corporate environmental performance.

The Financial Crisis and Governance Reform (2007–2008)

But the crises and scandals of the early 2000s were just the curtain-raiser for the main event: the Global Financial Crisis, or Great Recession of 2007–2008, the final wake-up call for corporate governance reform.[21]

- This financial meltdown, triggered by reckless risk-taking in banking and housing markets, exposed severe governance failures in financial institutions.

- The American global financial services firm Lehman Brothers collapsed, and governments bailed out major banks to prevent a global economic collapse.

- Public outrage over corporate excess, executive bonuses, and taxpayer-funded bailouts fuelled calls for stronger governance regulations.

In response, governments implemented reforms such as Dodd-Frank (USA) and Basel III (global banking regulations) to improve corporate accountability. Investors increasingly demanded transparency in corporate governance, further accelerating the ESG movement.

The Transition to a Sustainable Future

By the late 2000s, ESG had evolved from a theoretical concept into a global movement, driven by investors, regulators, and public expectations.

- The UN Sustainable Development Goals (SDGs), introduced in 2015, built on the progress of earlier frameworks, setting clear targets for global sustainability.

- The Paris Agreement on Climate Change (2015) further reinforced corporate responsibility in reducing emissions and transitioning to clean energy.

These global frameworks confirmed that ESG was no longer optional. It had become a central part of how businesses were expected to operate and how investors assessed risk and value.

The 2010s: ESG Goes Mainstream

With global frameworks in place, ESG moved from the margins to the mainstream in the 2010s. It became embedded in corporate strategy, investment criteria, and government policy. ESG reporting standards matured, and businesses of all sizes began to align their operations with ESG benchmarks. In 2011, less than one in five S&P 500 companies published a sustainability or ESG report. A decade later, that number had surged to over 90%, underscoring just how central ESG had become to corporate strategy and disclosure.

The shift wasn't just about avoiding risk—it was about seizing new opportunities. Companies that embraced ESG found themselves attracting investment, winning contracts, and retaining talent in ways that others could not.

This timeline highlights how CSR laid the philosophical groundwork for businesses' ethical obligations, while ESG evolved as a structured, measurable framework for sustainability and corporate accountability.

Time Period	Milestone/Era	Key Highlights
1600s	Origins of Joint-Stock Companies	Formation of British and Dutch East India Companies; early corporate purpose linked to national benefit and not just profit. Spark of CSR ideas emerge.
Late 1700s – Mid 1800s	Industrial Revolution and Exploitation	Massive industrial growth; rise of shareholder primacy; poor working conditions, child labour, debtors' prisons; early pushback begins.
1800s – Early 1900s	Robber Barons and Labour Reforms	Rise of monopolistic magnates; worker exploitation sparks labour unrest; early regulations and philanthropy (Carnegie's "Gospel of Wealth").
1930s – 1980s	Rise of CSR	Post-Depression shifts in corporate thinking; birth of CSR; post-WWII divergence between US shareholder model vs. European stakeholder model.
1950s – 1970s	CSR Gains Traction vs. Shareholder Focus	Key publications (e.g., Bowen's book), civil rights and environmental movements influence expectations; emergence of public accountability.
1980s – 1990s	Environmental Awareness & Voluntary CSR	UN and international environmental protocols (e.g., Rio Summit, Kyoto); CSR remains voluntary, but environmental and ethical concerns grow.
2000–2006	Birth of ESG	UN Global Compact (2000); "Who Cares Wins" report (2004); PRI launch (2006); shift from CSR to measurable ESG.
2000s	Corporate Scandals and Financial Crises	Enron, WorldCom, HIH, etc.; demand for stronger governance; ESG starts gaining traction as a risk management framework.
2010s	ESG Goes Mainstream	Paris Agreement & SDGs (2015); widespread ESG adoption and reporting; ESG tied to investment decisions and corporate performance.
2020s–Present	From Optional to Essential	ESG becomes core to strategy, compliance, and capital access; focus on sustainability, resilience, and stakeholder value intensifies.

2020s – Pushback?

Just as we were hoping that CSR and ESG had become an integral part of all business operations and planning, the world-wide political scene began to shift. Far-right parties had been established in some European countries for decades, but in the late 2010s, the United States joined in and brought renewed scepticism toward climate action, corporate accountability, and global cooperation.

This political pushback has complicated the ESG landscape, especially in regions where ESG is seen as "too political" or a threat to economic freedom.

Many companies have retreated from their previous embrace of ESG principles—in particular, from what is termed DEI in the United States (Diversity, Equity and Inclusion measures).[22] Some have opted for "greenhushing"—keeping their corporate heads below the parapets with non-committal statements. Add to that scepticism about (or active hostility to) environmental protection actions, and it would be easy to think that the robber barons and Milton Friedman have regained their omnipotence.

At the time of writing this book, we see such pushback as being confined to the US. Global companies that transact with the US (particularly those with government contracts) have altered their language but maintain their existing policies in other countries. They must choreograph a path between current US requirements and existing law in other jurisdictions. For example, Australia has legislation that covers many of the ESG big-ticket issues:

- Age Discrimination Act 2004
- Disability Discrimination Act 1992
- Racial Discrimination Act 1975
- Sex Discrimination Act 1984
- Australian Human Rights Commission Act 1986.

Codes of Conduct also exist that prevent Australian companies from abandoning equality (and other ESG-related activities).

Hence, we see the current resistance as yet another iteration of the ongoing ebb and flow of corporate responsibility. The underlying forces driving

ESG—climate risk, social expectation, and investor demand—remain strong and demand our attention as business owners and managers.

Chapter 3
The Reality Checks and Why ESG Matters

Rising Temperatures Leading to Rising Waters

Climate change isn't some far-off problem for future generations to deal with. It's here, now, and it's hitting small businesses where it hurts most—right in their communities, their supply chains, and their bottom lines.

A sustainable economy relies on a sustainable ecology

In March 2025, the St Vincent de Paul's Vinnies shop in Yarraman, a small town in Queensland northwest of Brisbane, closed permanently after severe floods devastated the region in late 2024. Streets turned into rivers, and homes and businesses alike were swallowed up by murky waters. The store had long served as a vital community hub and a source of low-cost goods, but the damage to its premises proved insurmountable. Despite community calls to reopen and widespread support for this beloved charity shop, the financial and logistical toll were too high. For many small operations like this rural Vinnies store, extreme events—amplified by climate change—don't just disrupt trade; they permanently erase livelihoods. Unlike larger businesses with reserves or insurance coverage, small enterprises often lack the reserves needed to recover. The closure of Yarraman's Vinnies reflects a growing reality: local economies are tethered to the health of their environment. As climate-related disasters become more frequent and intense, small businesses find themselves in a tenuous position, exposing the urgent needs for ESG strategies that counteract ecological instability.[23]

This weather event was part of a bigger pattern of increasingly severe storms and floods linked to global warming. For small businesses, extreme weather events are no longer a risk for the distant future; they are a reality today.

The Australian Bureau of Meteorology reports that the frequency of extreme weather events have increased significantly in the last 30 years, with more heatwaves, bushfires, and floods devastating businesses and communities. A 2022 study by Deloitte estimated that **climate-related disasters could cost the Australian economy \$100 billion annually by 2030**. Small businesses are disproportionately affected, as many lack the resources to recover from a major disruption.

What This Means for Australian SMEs:

✓ **Business continuity planning** – Small businesses need **resilience strategies**, such as flood-proofing premises, securing climate insurance, and ensuring supply chain redundancy.

✓ **Energy efficiency and emissions reduction** – Transitioning to **renewable energy and energy-efficient operations** can reduce costs while contributing to climate action.

✓ **Government incentives** – Programs like the **Australian Climate Solutions Package** offer funding for businesses investing in sustainable practices.

Synthetic Waste Impacting Organic Wildlife

Plastic is everywhere—in our packaging, our products and, unfortunately, our oceans. It's easy to think of plastic waste as someone else's problem, but the truth is, it's impacting communities and businesses in ways we might not expect.

Quality seafood relies on thriving oceans!

In Bali, the plastic pollution crisis has become a stark and daily reality. Beaches like Kuta and Seminyak, once international tourism hotspots, are now regularly blanketed in plastic bags, food wrappers, and broken household items. For local fishers and tourism operators, this isn't just an environmental issue; it's an economic emergency. Many now struggle to find fish in waters choked by debris. Tourists have taken notice too, with social media posts highlighting the jarring contrast between Bali's natural beauty and its mounting waste crisis. This decline in the island's image has had tangible consequences for the hospitality and retail sectors. These consequences were amplified during the Covid-19 pandemic when international tourism came to a halt. A hotel worker and long-time resident of Bali, Nyoman began organising local beach clean-ups during the lockdown. Partnering with grassroots initiatives such as One Island One Voice and Sungai Watch, he and other community members started removing hundreds of kilograms of plastic from the beaches each week. But the work didn't stop at clean-up. The community also began pushing for upstream solutions—educating residents about waste separation, advocating for reduced single-use plastics, and encouraging local businesses to adopt eco-friendly packaging and practices.

Their message was simple: sustainability isn't a luxury. It's a survival strategy. By actively restoring their environment, they hoped to rebuild their economy on more resilient, environmentally responsible foundations. For Nyoman and many others, these efforts were about more than tourism; they were about preserving the livelihoods and natural resources that generations of Balinese have relied on.[24]

Australia faces similar challenges. Every year, 130,000 tonnes of plastic waste leaks into Australia's environment, much of it ending up in our oceans. The Great Barrier Reef is experiencing increasing damage such as coral whitening and reducing marine life, all from plastic pollution, fisheries, and tourism.[25] For small businesses in industries like fishing, hospitality, and retail, sustainability is no longer optional; it's a business imperative.

What This Means for Australian SMEs:

✓ **Sustainable packaging and waste reduction** – The Australian government has set a target of **100% recyclable, reusable, or compostable packaging by 2025**. Small businesses should switch to biodegradable or reusable alternatives.

✓ **Reputation and consumer demand** – A 2023 Nielsen study found that **73% of Australian consumers prefer to buy from brands committed to sustainability**. Businesses that take a proactive stance can **win customer loyalty**.

✓ **Cost savings and compliance** – Reducing plastic waste can lower disposal costs and prepare businesses for stricter **state-based environmental regulations** in Australia

Children Labouring in Dirty Mines to Help Our Personalities Shine

When you hold your smartphone or laptop, do you ever think about where the materials inside it come from? The answer might surprise—and disturb—you.

Clean technologies depend on a thriving global workforce!

Meet Paul, a 14-year-old boy in the Democratic Republic of Congo. Instead of going to school, Paul spends his days in a cobalt mine, digging through the dirt with his bare hands—sometimes for more than 24 hours at a time—and suffers severe injuries and illness as a result. Cobalt and coltan from mines like Paul's end up in the batteries of smartphones and laptops sold worldwide.

When journalists exposed these conditions, consumers reacted with outrage. They didn't just target big tech companies; small electronics retailers and repair shops were caught in the crossfire too. Customers began demanding to know where products came from, and those businesses that couldn't answer faced a loss of trust—and sales.[26] This issue isn't far removed from Australia. The **Modern Slavery Act (2018)** requires large companies to report on forced labour risks in their supply chains, but small businesses aren't immune. Many SMEs supply **larger corporations that are now demanding full transparency from their partners.** Ethical sourcing is rapidly becoming a **competitive necessity**.

What This Means for Australian SMEs:

✓ **Ethical supply chains** – Australian businesses can **audit their suppliers** and prioritise sourcing from accredited, ethical suppliers (e.g., **Fairtrade, FSC-certified materials**).

✓ **Consumer and investor expectations** – Transparency in sourcing is now a **major factor in brand reputation** and can impact contracts with large buyers.

✓ **Legal and compliance risks** – Failing to address forced labour risks can result in penalties and exclusion from **government contracts.**

An Inclusive Workplace Embraces the Limits of Mind and Body

Inclusivity is a game-changer for businesses willing to embrace it. **More than just a human right, equal economic opportunity is also a business advantage.** When workplaces become accessible and inclusive, businesses benefit from increased innovation, stronger employee loyalty, and a broader talent pool.

The business ecosystem thrives when all people thrive!

Meet **Adam**, a young man with non-verbal autism. Before connecting with Hireup, traditional interviews and unaccommodating workplaces—

buffeted by high sensory demands and social expectations—made finding suitable employment nearly impossible. That changed when Hireup matched him with Trent, a support worker who understood Adam's unique needs and interests. Through their work together, Adam thrived in his new role, gained independence, and found meaningful engagement (Autism Awareness Australia. (2017, December 7). *A Hireup story of finding common ground: Adam and Trent* [Web post]. Autism Awareness Australia).

And guess what? **It wasn't just Adam who benefited; his employer did too**. Research shows that diverse workplaces drive h**igher innovation, stronger team performance, and better financial results**.[27]

This isn't just theory. The **Australian Bureau of Statistics** reports that people with disabilities aged 15–64 are **twice as likely to be unemployed** compared to those without disabilities. Companies that embrace diversity experience:

- **19% increase in revenue due to innovation**
- **30% higher employee retention rates, reducing hiring costs**
- **Greater customer loyalty, as consumers increasingly prefer brands that reflect inclusivity.**

What This Means for Australian SMEs:

✓ **Inclusive hiring for competitive advantage** – By actively hiring neurodiverse employees and people with disabilities, businesses **tap into unique skill sets** (e.g., attention to detail, analytical thinking, strong pattern recognition). Programs like the **National Disability Insurance Scheme (NDIS) Business Support** help SMEs implement inclusive hiring strategies

✓ **Legal and regulatory compliance** – The Disability Discrimination Act (1992) requires Australian businesses to provide reasonable workplace adjustments, making accessibility a legal and ethical priority.

✓ **Attracting talent and customers** – A 2023 Diversity Council Australia survey found that **78% of job seekers prefer working for inclusive employers**. Customers are also more likely to support businesses that demonstrate strong ESG values.

A Call to Action for SMEs

As Verna Myers, Vice President of Inclusion Strategy at Netflix, said: "Diversity is being invited to the party; inclusion is being asked to dance."

For SMEs, fostering an inclusive workplace goes beyond ensuring compliance. It's about **securing long-term success**. By embracing diverse hiring practices, creating accessible workspaces, and fostering a culture of belonging, businesses can **drive innovation, improve employee satisfaction, and enhance their reputation in a competitive market**.

Trafficked to Inflict Financial Havoc

We often think of online scams as annoying pop-ups or phishing emails. But what if these scams were connected to something far more sinister? **Human trafficking networks are increasingly linked to cybercrime**, where victims are forced to conduct online scams that target businesses, including small enterprises in Australia.

Robust financial controls stem the tide of nefarious ventures

Anika, a young woman from Myanmar, thought she was securing a job at a call centre in Cambodia. But when she arrived, she realised she'd been tricked. Her passport was confiscated, and she was forced to work long hours scamming people online. Anika's "job" was to send phishing emails and set up fake websites to steal money from unsuspecting victims, many of whom were small business owners in Australia.

In 2023, investigators uncovered a disturbing connection between cyber scams and human trafficking in Southeast Asia. Criminal syndicates were coercing trafficking victims like Anika to target small businesses through phishing attacks, fraudulent invoices, and ransomware scams.[28]

Small businesses account for 43% of cyberattacks globally due to their limited cybersecurity defences. Cybercrime also directly affects Australian businesses. The Australian Cyber Security Centre (ACSC) reported that cybercrime cost Australian businesses $33 billion in 2022 alone, with SMEs being the most affected.[29]

What This Means for Australian SMEs:

✓ **Strengthen cyber defences** – Small businesses should implement **multi-factor authentication, staff cyber security training, and secure payment gateways** to protect against scams.

✓ **Monitor supply chains** – Australian SMEs should conduct **due diligence on offshore suppliers and partners** to ensure they are not unknowingly connected to human rights violations or cyber fraud networks.

✓ **Government support and compliance** – The Australian government provides **cybersecurity grants and tax incentives** to help small businesses improve their digital security.

Phishing for Access and Control

Cybercrime isn't just a big business problem. Small businesses are prime targets because they typically have fewer defences in place. A single attack can destroy customer trust, disrupt operations, and lead to significant financial losses.

Securing all your digital assets is essential for agile businesses.

In April 2024, **T A Khoury & Co**, a small accounting firm in Sydney, was crippled by a ransomware attack carried out by the cybercriminal group **Hunters International.** Hackers locked the firm's systems and claimed to have stolen **over 63 GB of sensitive client and financial data**, demanding a ransom for its release. The breach forced the firm into crisis mode. Operations were halted, clients were notified, and trust was severely damaged. Some clients left, concerned about the safety of their financial records. The attack highlighted just how vulnerable small businesses are to cyber threats, especially those without robust cybersecurity measures.30

This experience is, unfortunately, not unique. The ACSC reports that ransomware attacks on Australian businesses increased by 75% in 2023, and the average cost of a data breach for SMEs is $200,000. Many businesses never recover from a major cyberattack.

What This Means for Australian SMEs:

✓ **Cyber Resilience Planning** – Every SME should have a **cybersecurity plan** that includes **regular data backups, employee training, and an incident response strategy.**

✓ **Protect Customer and Financial Data** – Using **encrypted networks, secure cloud storage, and antivirus software** reduces exposure to cyber risks.

✓ **Compliance with Australian Cybersecurity Standards** – The **Essential Eight Framework**[31] provides government-backed guidelines for **mitigating cyber threats.**

The Business Case for Cybersecurity

More than a mere IT issue, cybercrime is a critical business risk. SMEs must proactively protect their financial and digital assets to maintain client trust and ensure long-term sustainability.

Stronger cybersecurity reduces financial losses from fraud, ransomware, and phishing scams.

Investing in cybersecurity boosts business reputation and prevents customer churn.

Government incentives and compliance frameworks provide financial support for cybersecurity improvements.

As Francis Dinha, CEO of OpenVPN, stated: "Smaller businesses often don't realise just how vulnerable they are to cybercrime. It's true that these businesses don't have the same resources as larger corporations, but there's still plenty they can do to protect themselves."

For Australian SMEs, the question is no longer *if* they will face a cyber-attack, but *when*. Preparing today means securing tomorrow.

ESG Provides a Competitive Advantage for SMEs

ESG factors are about much more than mere ethics. They're about survival, reputation, and profitability. Whether it's protecting against climate risk, reducing waste, ensuring ethical sourcing, or embracing inclusivity, ESG means staying competitive.

By integrating ESG practices, small businesses can:

- Reduce long-term operational costs
- Gain access to grants, investment, and government incentives
- Build a resilient and future-proof business
- Enhance customer and employee loyalty

- Meet legal and regulatory expectations

Rather than seeing ESG as a burden, Australian SMEs should see it as an opportunity. We will explore this further in Chapter 7.

Chapter 4
Governance for SMEs

Foundations and Evolution

Governance (the G in ESG) is usually associated—especially in the minds of SME owners—with visions of board meetings with lots of people (mostly men) in sombre suits, intricate regulations, and complex policies. It is understandable then that governance can seem unnecessary. Bureaucracy for the sake of bureaucracy.

But governance is fundamental to every business, no matter its size. It's about ensuring your business is run well, sustainably, and with purpose. For SMEs, good governance can make the difference between surviving and thriving. In fact, the unacceptably high failure rate of small businesses is a direct consequence of poor governance and management.

So, while it doesn't require the complexity of large corporations, SME governance does require attention. The good news? You don't need to feel overwhelmed. By starting small and focusing on the basics, you can build a framework that grows with your business and supports its success.[32]

This chapter will explain:

- What governance actually is
- What you need to do
- Where to start

We'll explore the practical steps SMEs can take to implement governance systems that grow with their business, and we'll address some specific SME risks.

For SMEs, good governance does not mean mirroring what a multinational company does. Unfortunately, though, much of the advice and material available to SMEs is exactly that—a scaled-down version of what is used at the big end of town. It's no wonder that overwhelm is a common response. This mini-corporate approach ignores so much of what an SME is—its size, risks, capabilities, cash resources, available time...

What Is Governance?

At its heart, governance refers to how decisions are made, implemented, and monitored within a business. It's the framework that ensures accountability, transparency, and ethical behaviour in all aspects of operations. While governance is sometimes dismissed as "red tape", it is, in fact, the scaffolding that allows businesses to thrive in a sustainable and ethical manner. Done well, governance can improve decision-making, reduce risk, and position your business for success in an increasingly competitive and regulated environment.

Good governance operates on 4 key principles:

1. **Transparency** – clear communication and openness about decisions
2. **Accountability** – defining who is responsible for what
3. **Fairness** – treating all stakeholders equitably
4. **Responsibility** – meeting ethical standards and complying with laws

For SMEs, this usually begins with the owner. It is their vision and decisions that shape the culture and purpose of the business. Unlike larger corporations with extensive resources, SMEs rely heavily on the owner's leadership and values to embed governance into the day-to-day operations.

For SMEs, these principles often play out in more informal ways than in large corporations, especially at the beginning of their business evolution. Yet their importance remains the same.

In practice, this means having:

- Clear roles and responsibilities
- Documented policies and procedures
- Financial oversight and risk management
- Compliance and ethical standards[33]

Financial oversight and compliance are no-brainers. They're required by law. For many SMEs, documented policies, procedures, and ethical standards are also legal requirements (depending on what industry you operate in), so if you are operating according to the law, your governance is largely under control.

It's not that difficult!

Governance for SMEs vs. Large Corporations

In large corporations, governance frameworks are typically formalized, with clear distinctions between ownership, management, and oversight. These frameworks are designed to address what is known as the "principal-agent problem", where the interests of owners (principals) may not align with those of managers (agents).

SMEs, however, operate differently. In most cases, the owner is also the manager, making decisions and setting the direction for the business. This overlap means that governance in SMEs focuses less on oversight and more on structure, culture, and risk management.

Governance in SMEs focuses less on oversight and more on structure, culture, and risk management.

While the absence of formal governance structures might work in the short term, it can create vulnerabilities as the business grows. Without clear policies and procedures, SMEs may struggle with inefficiencies, conflicts, or even compliance issues. For example, an SME operating without a cybersecurity plan could fall victim to a data breach, damaging its reputation and customer trust. Similarly, a lack of financial controls might lead to poor cash flow management, jeopardizing the business's stability.

Governance and the Law

All Australian companies, including small businesses, are governed by the Corporations Act and its associated regulations. The legislation is administered by the Australian Securities and Investments Commission (ASIC), so all companies must be registered with ASIC.

The over-arching governance responsibility for all company directors is to act "in the best interests of the corporation". In practice, this means considering the long-term future of the business, not just short-term profits or advantages for the owner.[34]

Governance through the SME Growth Journey

Governance isn't static; it evolves as a business grows and its needs become more complex. Using the stages from the *Small Company, Big Business* Business Journey framework, we can understand how governance requirements change over time and how SMEs can adapt.

Startup Phase: Laying the Foundations

In the early days of a business, the focus is on survival. Typically, the owner is involved in every aspect of the business, from sales and marketing to operations and finance. Governance at this stage is informal, with decisions made on the fly and documented sparingly, if at all.

Pushing classic corporate governance demands onto SMEs at this stage is neither helpful nor welcome. Time and money are in short supply, and the founder will typically resist giving up any decision-making power. A notable exception, however, is the startup seeking early-stage capital. In that case, investors will be looking for robust governance arrangements even at this early stage.

While this flexibility is necessary for a startup, certain elements of governance must still be addressed. The International Finance Corporation calls these "pre-governance" issues.

1. **Defining purpose**: What is your business's mission? This purpose acts as a North Star, guiding decisions and ensuring consistency in operations. For example, a small bakery might define its purpose as providing high-quality, sustainably sourced products to the local community.

2. **Building culture**: Even in a one-person business, culture matters. Setting standards for ethics, customer service, and decision-making lays the groundwork for future growth.

3. **Managing risks**: Startups often overlook risks altogether. (SME owners are naturally optimistic!) But that approach is a shortcut to a business's demise. There are also some risks that SMEs ignore, presuming they're too small to be targeted. A classic example is cybersecurity. A single phishing email can lead to significant financial and reputational damage.

For the small startup, governance will probably mean contact with a limited number of external advisors—certainly an accountant, and probably a lawyer. Perhaps there is an informal connection to a business advisor. Everyone knows what they're supposed to do, but it probably isn't written down. The legal requirements are covered, pretty much, but not a lot beyond this.

Growth Phase: Building Structures

As the business grows, so does its complexity. More employees, clients and processes mean more decisions—and a greater need for structure.

During this phase, governance begins to formalize:

- **Policies and procedures**: Basic financial controls, HR policies, and operational guidelines are introduced to ensure consistency and reduce risks. Organisation charts, recruitment priorities, insurances, codes of conduct, branding and marketing start to emerge.

- **Formal external advisors**: Trusted advisors, beyond the accountant and lawyer, are present. The owner may even establish an advisory board, a group of trusted people who provide guidance.

- **Decision-making**: Instead of the owner/founder taking responsibility for all decisions, it may be shared amongst some senior team members. Some decisions may be delegated.

Stabilization Phase: Strengthening Foundations

In the stabilization phase, the business has reached a level of operational maturity. The business structure is stable, with defined levels of management responsibility. The business has a clear vision of who it exists to serve, how, and why. Governance becomes more strategic, focusing on long-term sustainability and risk management. The business has become a saleable asset, and potential purchasers will be looking closely at everything to do with governance, not just the financials.

Key developments include:

- **Formal governance structures**: This might include establishing a board of directors or at least a board of advisors.

- **Internal controls**: Comprehensive policies and procedures continue to be developed. Risk management plans, workplace safety plans, quality plans, and compliance processes are now needed.

- **Stakeholder reporting**: Regular updates to investors, customers, and employees build trust and demonstrate accountability.

Expansion Phase: Embracing Complexity

In the expansion phase, businesses often enter new markets or scale their operations significantly. Governance must now accommodate a more diverse set of stakeholders and challenges.

Key governance developments are:

- **Transparency and reporting**: Clear, detailed reporting becomes critical for securing investment and maintaining trust. Government-required reporting obligations also increase. If the company decides to be listed on the stock market, a tsunami of legal requirements arises.

- **Stakeholder engagement**: Actively involving employees, customers, and communities in decision-making processes can strengthen relationships and enhance reputation. The company directors can expect increased scrutiny from their various stakeholders, and the company must have the ability to satisfy that level of inspection.

The clear message here is not to dismiss the G in ESG as another time-wasting and costly thing you have to do. There are certainly some wasteful requirements, but overall, good governance is your business's best defence mechanism.

The Four-Stage Governance Journey

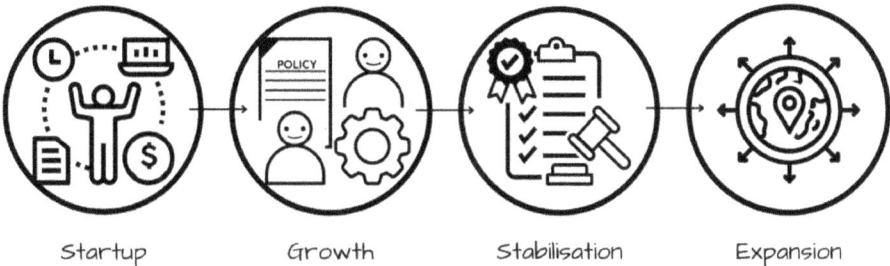

| Startup | Growth | Stabilisation | Expansion |

An Extra Note: The Role of Cybersecurity and AI in Modern Governance

Any SME faces multiple risks. Robust risk management is required. Again, it doesn't have to be overwhelming, as Bronwyn has described in her 2022 bestselling book Small Company, Big Crisis. However, we need to point out two of the most significant governance challenges (and opportunities) for SMEs today: cybersecurity and AI.

Cybersecurity:

- **Risks**: Data breaches, phishing attacks, and ransomware can disrupt operations and erode trust.

- **Solutions**: Basic protections, such as firewalls and secure passwords, should be in place from the start. As the business grows, more advanced measures, like regular audits and incident response plans, become necessary.

AI:

- **Opportunities**: AI can streamline operations, improve decision-making, and enhance customer service.

- **Risks**: Misuse of AI can lead to ethical issues, privacy violations, and reputational damage. SMEs must approach AI adoption with caution, ensuring transparency and compliance with relevant laws.

Although we are not qualified in these areas ourselves, we have worked with a number of experts over the years in the process of helping our clients. You are very welcome to tap into our networks by simply reaching out to us.

We urge you to address these risks in the early stages of your business, or you might not have a business at all.

Good governance calls for thoughtful planning and incremental improvements. In this way, SMEs can navigate their business growth confidently, setting the stage for long-term success. It's not about replicating the practices of large corporations; it's about starting with the basics and building on them as the business grows. By focusing on purpose, culture, and risk management from the beginning, SMEs can create a governance framework that evolves with their needs but doesn't overwhelm them.

Practical Steps for SMEs:

1. Start with advisors: Lean on external professionals like accountants or consultants for initial guidance.

2. Focus on culture and purpose: Build a business ethos centred on ethics, transparency, and customer value.

3. Prioritise risk management: Address key risks like cybersecurity early, even if your business is small.

Resource

The authors have written a basic Governance Plan. Of course, no one plan can fulfil every company's needs, but AI prompts are included to customise the plan to your business. (IT'S FOR SALE, NOT FREE.)

Chapter 5
ESG and Risk Management – Building Resilience for SMEs

Risk management isn't a comfortable topic for many small business owners. Often, it's something that sits on the back burner—until a crisis hits. And when it does, businesses scramble to contain the damage, often realising too late that with better preparation the crisis could have been prevented or at least mitigated.

ESG is no longer just about compliance; it's about resilience. It's about ensuring that your business can withstand and adapt to the growing number of environmental, social, and governance-related risks that are reshaping industries and economies, and even capitalise upon those risks.

SMEs often don't have any risk management processes in place, partly because traditional risk management frameworks—those designed for large corporations—feel unwieldy and impractical for smaller businesses.

Now, enter ESG (Environmental, Social, and Governance).

For years, ESG was something that only large corporations worried about, a set of compliance requirements, sustainability reports, and investor-driven policies that seemed distant from the realities of running a small business.

ESG is no longer just about compliance;
it's about resilience.

For SMEs, ESG risk management isn't just about avoiding regulatory penalties or meeting supplier/customer/employee/financier expectations. It's about securing long-term business stability and positioning the company for future growth. This chapter explores why ESG and risk management must be integrated, how SMEs can approach ESG-related risks in a practical way, and what steps SMEs can take to build resilience in a world that increasingly values sustainability and ethical business practices.

The Intersection of ESG and Risk Management

Risk management is about identifying potential threats and taking action to minimise their impact. Traditionally, this has focused on financial, operational, and market risks. But ESG introduces new dimensions to risk that SMEs can no longer afford to ignore.

Consider the following examples:

- **Environmental risks**: Extreme weather events, rising energy costs, stricter emissions regulations or a global pandemic can disrupt business operations and increase expenses.

- **Social risks**: A small business caught up in a labour rights controversy—whether directly or through its suppliers—faces reputational damage that could be difficult to recover from.

- **Governance risks**: Fraud, corruption, and lack of transparency can lead to legal troubles, loss of investor confidence, and broken business relationships.

Ignoring these risks doesn't make them disappear. In fact, the biggest risk SMEs face with ESG is the risk of inaction. Waiting until ESG factors become a problem is the same as waiting until the roof collapses before fixing a leak. It's far more expensive, disruptive, and damaging than addressing the issue early.

That's why integrating ESG into risk management isn't just a matter of compliance. It's a business imperative. There isn't such a thing as "ESG risk management". There's just risk management that includes ESG risks.

Why SMEs Need to Rethink Their Approach to Risk Management

Traditionally, SMEs have taken an informal, reactive approach to risk management. When a problem arises, they deal with it. When a supplier fails, they find a new one. When a compliance issue emerges, they scramble to fix it.

But ESG-related risks are different. They tend to be long-term, systemic, and interconnected. Climate risks, for example, will affect more than one supplier; they can disrupt entire supply chains. Governance failures lead not only to fines, but they also erode trust and can permanently damage a business's reputation.

This means that SMEs need to shift from a reactive mindset to a proactive, structured approach to risk. Fortunately, this doesn't require complex corporate frameworks or overwhelming processes and lots of jargon. It simply requires SMEs to take a structured, thoughtful approach to identifying, assessing, and mitigating risks.

In Small Company, Big Crisis, Bronwyn outlines a risk management process that is widely used by SMEs because it is practical and straightforward, and it doesn't require a team of compliance officers to implement. The same process can be adapted for ESG risks.

Practical Steps for SMEs to Integrate ESG into Risk Management

A risk management process doesn't have to be complicated, but it does need to be structured. Here's how SMEs can integrate ESG into their existing risk management practices using a simple and effective risk management assessment approach:

Step 1: Identify ESG Risks

The first step is to identify what ESG risks are relevant to the business. This means asking questions like:

- How might climate change impact my supply chain or operations?
- Are we actively working to reduce our environmental footprint?
- Are there any labour or human rights risks in my workforce or supplier base?
- Is our workplace safe?
- Are we using more packaging than we need to, which ends up in landfill?
- Are our promotional products ending up in landfills?
- Do we contribute to our local community, either as a company or as individuals?
- Are we complying with all relevant regulations on governance and ethics?
- Have we protected the company against fraud, either by an employee or an outside party?
- Could our customers' data be stolen or compromised?
- Are we at risk of reputational damage due to ESG-related issues?
- Are we making claims about our products being sustainable/eco-friendly/green that we cannot prove?
- Does our company culture encourage ethical behaviour at all times?
- Is our company's intellectual property in jeopardy due to being used to train and improve AI models?

Some SMEs conduct informal risk assessments, while others bring in external consultants for a more detailed review. Either way, the goal is to create a clear picture of where the business is vulnerable. List all the identified risks in a table. This will be the beginnings of your business Risk Management Plan.

Step 2: Assess and Prioritise

Not all risks are equally likely to occur. (If your Australian business is in the northern Queensland city of Cairns, you are much more likely to encounter a cyclone than a bushfire.) Similarly, not all events will have a similar impact if they do occur. Some are an inconvenience, and some are more severe. A simple way to assess and prioritise ESG risks is to use a Risk Matrix. A Risk Matrix asks you to think about the risks you face, then rate them on:

- **Likelihood** – How likely is it that this risk will materialise?

- **Impact** – If this risk does materialise, how severe will the consequences be?

LIKELIHOOD	CONSEQUENCE				
	Insignificant	Minor	Moderate	Major	Catastrophic
ALMOST CERTAIN	High	High	Extreme	Extreme	Extreme
LIKELY	Medium	High	High	Extreme	Extreme
OCCASIONAL	Low	Medium	High	Extreme	Extreme
UNLIKELY	Low	Low	Medium	High	Extreme
RARE	Low	Low	Medium	High	High

The Risk Matrix helps you to prioritise where you spend your time and resources. For example, an SME operating in a drought-prone region might identify water shortages as Almost Certain to happen, with Major consequences. Thus, the risk of water shortages is an Extreme risk for the company, and action needs to be taken to mitigate the risk. Anything that has an Extreme risk level should be dealt with first – even if they are the most difficult.

Step 3: Develop Mitigation Strategies

Once the key ESG risks have been identified and prioritised, the next step is to develop mitigation strategies; that is, what you are going to do to:

- help prevent the event from happening at all
- reduce the impact if it does happen
- recover after the event has happened

A simple example of how this works is shown below.

EVENT	CHANCE OF IT HAPPENING	IMPACT IF IT HAPPENS	HOW IT IS MANAGED
E: Insurance costs increase	Almost certain	Moderate: Reduced cash flow Disrupt normal operations Need to borrow funds	Liaise with insurers to demonstrate proactive measures to reduce flood/fire/cyclone etc.
S: Serious safety incident due to poor working conditions	Likely	Catastrophic if a death or permanent injury occurs	Robust, implemented WHS Systems Trained team
G: Loss of data or hacking	Unlikely	Major: Cannot operate Lose clients Out of business	Back-ups, IT Maintenance & Redundancy

Note: Between 2022 and 2023, the average home insurance premium in Australia rose by 14%, the biggest rise in a decade, so it's a real risk for all Australian SMEs.[35]

These strategies/plans don't have to be complex, but they do need to be actionable and prepared in advance. If you have ever been on the receiving end of one of these risk events—a cyclone, fire, flood, cyber-attack, serious injury or death at the workplace—you will know the feeling of being overwhelmed. Making decisions in these circumstances is difficult, or even impossible. The saying "frozen like a rabbit in the headlights" describes how you will probably feel.

However, if plans have been made and communicated in advance, your business doesn't have to fall victim to whatever it is that has gone wrong. You may not have been completely accurate in foreseeing the event and its consequences, but some planning is infinitely better than none.

To get your own Risk Management Plan started, check out some of the resources linked from page (CTA).

Step 4: Assign Responsibility and Embed ESG in Decision-Making

It is no use taking the time and mental resources required to complete this process if the plan is simply stored away on a server somewhere. Risk management fails when no one is responsible for it. For SMEs, this often means that the business owner or a senior leader (an ESG Champion) must take ownership of ESG risks.

We noted earlier that "ESG risk" isn't a thing. There's just risk—and some of it comes from ESG-related hazards. It's the same with decision-making. ESG topics need to be a part of all decisions. For example:

- Supplier selection criteria should include ESG performance.
- Hiring and HR policies should consider diversity and fair treatment.
- Investment decisions should factor in sustainability risks.
- ESG training should be provided to employees, so they understand their role in managing these risks. If your business is a family

business, the younger generation is highly likely to be motivated by ESG issues. More on this topic in Chapter 9: Integrating ESG into Business Strategy.

Risk management is not a one-time activity. It's an ongoing process that requires regular reviews to make sure your plan is still relevant. It's a good idea to schedule a review into your calendar. We all know how things that aren't urgent can slip to the bottom of the To Do list, but here are some suggestions for things you should include in your reviews:

- How are you performing? Track ESG risk indicators, such as energy consumption, employee turnover, or compliance violations. Chapter 6 gives guidance on how you can measure and report on your ESG impacts.

- Do any changes in local conditions have implications for your plans?[36]

- Have any legislation/regulations or industry trends changed?

- Are there any updated forecasts that would help with your planning?[37]

- Regular review will help keep your risk management plan current. Avoid being taken by surprise.

A word about two major risks: Cybersecurity and AI

Who knows what risks AI may pose to businesses? Here we have outlined the obvious ones that have already proven they can create havoc. The list is by no means definitive, and we have a lot more to learn about AI and Cybersecuity yet.

AI overreliance and inaccuracy

The most commonly known risk with Chat GPT is the concept of "hallucinations", where the AI states information as if it were factual, and the user starts to rely on the information provided.

Explainability and transparency

Lack of explainability and transparency over the algorithmic outputs, which could lead to over-reliance on unreliable predictions, impacting business decisions.

Systematic bias

Large language models such as ChatGPT are trained using publicly available data, subjecting the platform to inherent systematic biases such as racist or sexist biases being programmed into the machines.

Data protection and security

Foundational models are noted to have memorisation capabilities which may result in the unintentional sharing of sensitive/confidential data, exposing users to privacy and (General Data Protection Regulation) GDPR violations.

Audit and Regulation

While AI-specific regulation has yet to arrive, irresponsible usage of AI may adversely impact an organisation's current regulatory obligation.

The Cost of Doing Nothing

ESG risk management is no longer just for big corporations with compliance teams and investor obligations. It's a critical business practice for SMEs that want to remain resilient, competitive, and future-proof.

Choosing not to address ESG risks is, in itself, a decision, with real and often costly consequences. **The biggest ESG risk isn't regulatory fines, reputational damage, or supply chain disruptions. It's doing nothing at all.** The cost of inaction is almost always higher than the cost of prevention.

The biggest ESG risk isn't regulatory fines,
reputational damage, or supply chain disruptions.
It's doing nothing at all

Chapter 6
Measurement and Tracking the Impact of ESG

Several years ago, I (Stephen) was part of a small team that visited communities in Northern Sulawesi, Indonesia, that our local Australian community supported through the Bridge of Hope initiative. One project involved sponsoring around 25 internally displaced families who had been granted plots of land on a hillside. Their goal was to terrace, irrigate, and transform the land into a village of new homes and farms.

On our first visit in mid-2008, we met these families—about 150 people in total—who were gathered inside a community hall no larger than a typical three-bedroom house, close to the forest-covered land they would soon cultivate. After introductions, our team sat with the family heads to discuss their plans and the support they might need. They lacked clear answers and seemed without essential skills, tools, or resources for the task. One of our team members, an engineer, began offering detailed recommendations on how to proceed, even envisioning designs to help them plan.

A year later, our team returned to see what progress had been made. To our surprise, and without any external intervention, the community had fully cleared and irrigated the land, creating a terraced village complete with a central path and rows of timber houses. I was struck by the ingenuity and resilience of these people who, despite limited resources, had achieved so much. This experience left a lasting impression about the nature of social impact and how to measure it.

In this chapter we take a look at how small businesses can measure and track the impact of their ESG efforts on people and the planet, and how to put the necessary governance structures in place. This chapter will cover setting short- and long-term goals, introduce metrics to gauge progress, and review some useful tools for monitoring and reporting impact. As our story suggests, practical advice on ensuring that ESG initiatives truly deliver is essential.

"Not everything that counts can be counted, and not everything that can be counted, counts."

—*William Bruce Cameron, Sociologist*

Small business owners who aim to make an impact in ESG must be able to quantify their impact to show the immediate social and environmental outcomes of their strategy. From a business perspective, it provides a way to account for investments (in time and resources), track internal improvements, and demonstrate commitment externally. According to Spark Strategy, impact measurement can increase investments and partnerships, differentiate you from competitors, and showcase your company's value, while also increasing transparency and strengthening decision-making.[38] In short, measuring impact is about proving that ESG efforts are effective, guiding resource allocation and engaging employees and customers in meaningful ways.

Before we dive into the steps for measuring impact, it's essential to clarify:

- What you want to achieve
- How you intend to achieve it
- Why it is important to you.

The first question addresses motivation. Impact Frontiers refers to the ABC of impact investing: Avoid, Benefit, or Contribute.[39] Are we aiming to avoid risks to the business, provide benefits to a community, or contribute to a broader impact?

The ABC of Impact Investing

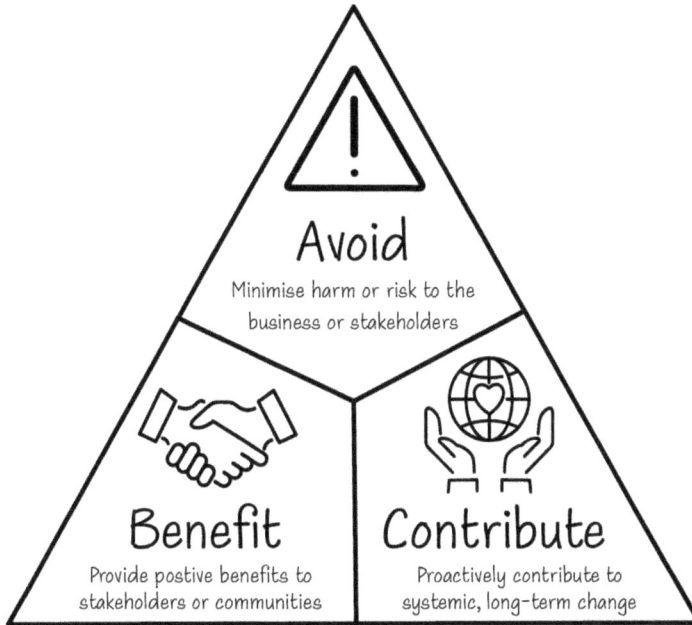

Avoid
Minimise harm or risk to the business or stakeholders

Benefit
Provide postive benefits to stakeholders or communities

Contribute
Proactively contribute to systemic, long-term change

Source Adapted from Impact Frontiers

The second question considers what we can realistically achieve and our role in reaching that goal. Think of our opening story—what role did our team play? Our influence was indirect, expressed through our relationship with Bridge of Hope, local Indonesian nationals dedicated to their work. Our contributions were based on years of friendship and financial support.

Setting Your ESG Preferred Future and Goals

With these principles in mind, let's discuss how to establish a framework for measuring impact. Start by defining what you want to achieve, and envision a preferred future for your business. Reflect on the ESG aspects discussed earlier, and consider the main ways your business can benefit its environment and community. Keep in mind that this goes beyond legal compliance or client expectations; it's about the impact of your business and how its practices can improve.

With that clear vision, establish both short- and long-term goals, recognizing that true impact takes time. Setting ESG goals and objectives is the first step toward effective impact measurement. Objectives should address both immediate needs and long-term aspirations, enabling the business to make incremental progress toward broader aims.

Here are some prompts to kick-start your thought process.

1. Identifying Key Areas of Positive Impact

Key impact areas include:

- Ethical sourcing: changes in purchasing choices and product ingredients
- Capacity building: growth in skills and knowledge
- Partnerships: collaborations for shared impact
- Advocacy: helping to shape public policy
- Transparency: openly sharing actions and values
- Grievance mechanisms: responsiveness to concerns
- Innovation: investing in new technologies or methods

2. Short-Term Goals Focused on Immediate Impact

Short-term goals often focus on measurable actions that don't require extensive resources. For instance, a 10% reduction in energy use or increasing workforce diversity are achievable, quick-win goals that also provide data points for refining future efforts.

3. Long-Term Goals for Strategic Development

Long-term goals aim for transformational impact, like achieving net-zero emissions or creating a supply chain free from forced labour. Drawing on frameworks such as the UN Sustainable Development Goals (SDGs) can help you align these goals with global standards. Revisiting goals periodically allows your business to stay agile in its ESG journey as circumstances evolve.

How to Measure Success: Theory Change and Logic Model

Below we describe a model you can use to help set your goals, work out what you need in order to achieve them, and measure your success.

Theory of Change

Through doing Activity **X**	We will address Social Issue **Y**	Achieving Outcome **Z**
What activities are you conducting for the project?	What is the social issue you are addressing?	What are the intended outcomes for your project?

1. Theory of Change

Creating a theory of change is a helpful way to zoom out on your activity and get back to the basics. It is a clear and concise way to lay out your big picture plan and can help keep all your staff on the same page. Developing a "Theory of Change" methodology will help you define the change you aim to make, clarifying the link between activities and impact. For instance, your focus on social impact might state: "Through offering vocational training programs, we address local unemployment and enhance workforce diversity." Put simply, through doing activity X, we will address social issue Y and achieve outcome Z. This structure clarifies the purpose of each initiative, providing a clear goalpost for measurement.[40]

2. Logic Model Template

It's from this Theory of Change method that you can then use a logic model template to map out all the activities you aim to measure. To help you visualise this, let's imagine you are standing by the side of a pond. You pick up a stone and throw it into the centre of the pond. Naturally, the stone makes an initial splash in the water and from there the waves of that impact ripple out towards the pond's edges. In this sequence, we can map out the logic of what happened:

1. Activity: throwing the stone
2. Input: you and the stone
3. Indicator: the intensity of the splash and/or frequency of ripples
4. Output: the splash created by the stone
5. Outcome: initial ripples from the splash
6. Impact: outer ripples

Though not a perfect illustration, it shows how a simple logic model works.

1. The activity is what you are doing to make an impact.
2. The input is the resources needed for the activity/program.
3. The indicator is the metric used to represent your impact by quantity or by quality.
4. The output is the immediate results of the program.
5. The outcome is the short-term to medium-term results.
6. The impact is the end of the program outcome/long-term results.

◄——— Planned Work ———►			◄——— Intended Results ———►		
Activities	**Inputs**	**Indicators**	**Outputs**	**Outcome**	**Impact**
The activity is what you do to achieve your desired impact. Including the workshops and resources created for the program.	Inputs are what you bring to the table. They are the resources necessary for the activity to run.	The metric used to represent your impact. This can represent quantitative and/or qualitative data.	Outputs are the direct results of the activity you carried out. e.g. the steps taken to measure the activity.	Outcomes are changes you expect to see in short to medium-term as a consequence of your activities.	Impact is the long-term impact of your program or the change (intended or unintended) occurring to individuals, communities, systems as a result of your program.

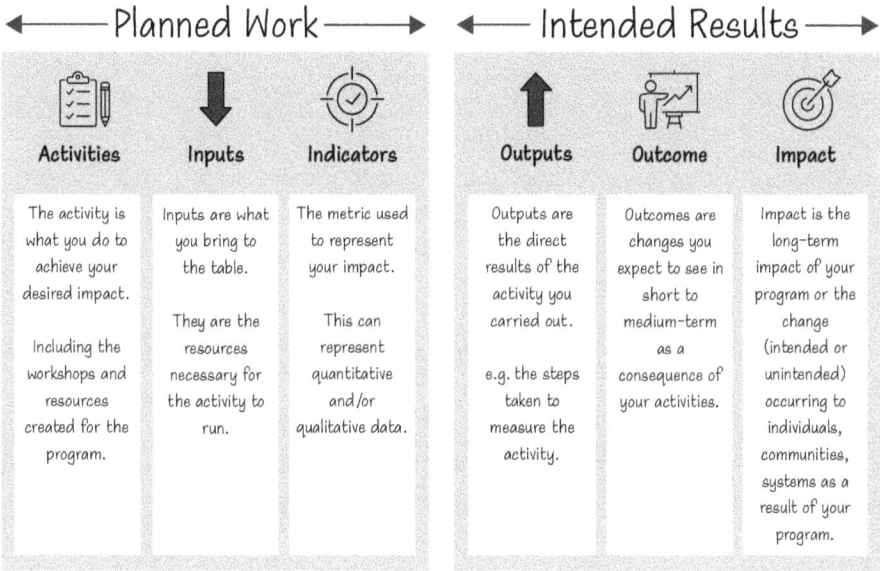

When we apply this to business:

1. Identifying Key Inputs

Inputs are the resources and processes SMEs bring to their ESG initiatives. In the context of environmental sustainability, inputs might include the funds allocated to renewable energy upgrades or employee time dedicated to sustainability training. For social goals, inputs could involve partnerships with local community organizations.

2. Activities and Immediate Outputs

Activities represent the core actions taken to address ESG objectives, such as implementing energy-saving measures or conducting training sessions. Initial results from the immediate outputs provide the basis for evaluating effectiveness. For instance, an SME aiming to reduce waste might measure the weight of recycled materials as an immediate output, helping to gauge the short-term impact of its waste reduction program.

Sample Activities: Specific actions like waste audits, diversity training, or energy audits.

Sample Outputs: Direct results, such as "10 employees trained" or "5% reduction in plastic waste".

Short- and Medium-Term Outcomes

Outcomes measure the broader impact of ESG activities over time, indicating whether the organization is on track to meet its goals. Short-term outcomes for a diversity initiative might include an increase in underrepresented groups within the workforce. For environmental goals, a decrease in monthly energy consumption compared to the previous year reflects ongoing progress.

Sample Outcomes: Broader effects, including increased employee engagement or decreased energy usage.

Long-Term Impact and End Goals

The goal of impact measurement is to determine the long-term effects of ESG activities, often extending beyond the company itself to influence industry standards or community well-being. For example, reducing emissions can contribute to improved air quality, while a successful diversity initiative can create a more inclusive workplace culture. For an SME focusing on social impact, an activity might involve conducting diversity and inclusion training. The outputs would then be the number of employees trained, while the outcome could be higher diversity in new hires. Long term, the impact would be a more inclusive workplace that attracts talent from diverse backgrounds.

A logic model provides a structured way to capture the cause-and-effect relationship between activities and outcomes. This model, often visualized as a chain of events from inputs to impact, can guide SMEs in tracking their progress:

"Transition to sustainable packaging"

- **Activity**: Switching to biodegradable materials for packaging
- **Input**: Resources allocated to sustainable packaging initiatives
- **Indicator:** Percentage of plastic usage reduced
- **Output**: Reduction in plastic usage by 20% over six months
- **Outcome**: Decreased environmental impact, measured by reduced landfill contributions

- **Impact**: Enhanced brand reputation and increased customer loyalty due to sustainable practices[41]

The Nuts and Bolts of Impact Measurement

Now that we've got the overarching impact measurement framework in place to track your progress (Theory of Change and Logic Model Template), we can now get to the nuts and bolts of what is going to go into this framework to build it out for each activity. The following questions serve as a guide and will help you to apply your logic model more concretely:

- **Deciding on the right measurement indicators:** number and value

You will have noticed that in the Logic Model section above, we didn't discuss what indicators to apply to measure the chain of events following an activity. We've placed it here in Nuts and Bolts simply to give it more focussed attention. When measuring impact, it's very common for businesses to measure what we are doing by number or quantity. When it comes to environmental impact areas, we can count things like the number of resources used, emitted, and wasted (greenhouse gases, single use plastics, etc). We can represent this data by percentage, ratio, and proportion to describe what is happening with tangible things.

"You can't manage what you can't measure."

—Peter Drucker, management consultant

However, impact measurement is more than what we can count by number. It's also about what we can count by quality or qualitatively. This is especially true when we are measuring what is happening for and within people. When it comes to social impact, we need to consider output and outcomes by perception, behaviour, skill, satisfaction, and quality.

As an example, we could roll out a training program for our team on how to phase out single-use plastics from our packaging. By quantity (quantitively) we could measure that 15 out of 20 people completed the training program, or 75%. By quality, we could then measure the change of behaviour that occurred: following the training, 5 of the 15 people who completed the training program formed a focus group to discuss ways in which the company could reduce its reliance on single-use plastics and identified ways they could do so personally.

As you experiment with this, you may find that two or more indicators might be necessary to prove impact. It might also be necessary to include mixed methods for each indicator (qualitative and quantitative).

Deciding on what you can measure and have an impact on

We mentioned earlier in the chapter that not everything you may wish to see changed can be changed by you. It may also be the case that the steps we take may have unintended consequences and may trigger outcomes we didn't expect. As we've already seen in this book, the world of ESG reporting is enormous and very complex. As such we will be limited in what we can hope to achieve. Consider a large company based in an office tower in Sydney that reports under the Australian Modern Slavery Act. One of their goals is to "reduce the number of modern slavery enquiries referred to the organisation". This type of goal is too broad to provide any insight into how the individual activity would be of benefit. In addition to being a broad goal, it is also unrealistic, given the distance between the main operations of this company and where a case of modern slavery might be found.

We also need to be aware of the danger of simply measuring what's easiest to count. This is the most common reason for those unintended consequences. Consider a regional local council in a large agricultural precinct deciding to educate local farmers on how to be more effective in water management. Sensing the difficulty of bringing all the farmers together at the town hall to discuss the issue, the council decides to develop and distribute pamphlets to all residences, hoping this will get the word out. If all that the council measured and reported on was the number of pamphlets given out, this would not give any indication of changes in understanding (metric: perception) of the issues and any changes in water management (metric: behaviour). You get what you measure.

Given this, as you start applying your logic model to certain activities, it is important to keep in mind the following four principles:

- **Correlation**: Ensure at least one indicator is linked to your area of impact; e.g., if your poster is impacting a growth in awareness, you need to measure how knowledge has grown since the distribution of the resource.

- **Specificity**: The point of these indicators is to establish whether your activity is effective in its intended purpose. It is difficult to prove causality to broad outcomes.

- **Logical**: Make sure that your indicators correlate logically to your activities, outputs, and outcomes.

- **Realistic**: Ask yourself, is it possible to capture this information?

Tools for Reporting ESG Performance

Once objectives and metrics are set, reporting becomes essential. SMEs can use accessible tools and frameworks to communicate their impact, ensuring transparency and fostering trust.

- **Affordable technology solutions for SMEs**
  Several affordable or free digital tools, such as Microsoft Excel or Google Sheets, are suitable for tracking ESG data and creating visual reports. More advanced software like Ecochain or Planetly may also offer specialized tracking capabilities for a moderate cost, providing automated calculations and scenario analysis that can enhance data reliability.

- **Third-party certifications**
  Certification bodies such as B Corp, Fair Trade, or ISO 14001 for environmental management provide SMEs with verified benchmarks, enhancing credibility in their ESG reporting. These certifications often come with pre-defined indicators and reporting structures, making it easier for smaller businesses to communicate their impact in recognized formats.

Building a Measurement Culture

Effective ESG impact measurement depends on a strong internal culture that values accountability and continuous improvement.

- **Establish an executive sponsor and team champions**
  Building a measurement culture begins with leadership buy-in. Appointing an executive sponsor and engaging champions within the company can drive momentum and ensure sustained focus on ESG objectives.

- **Encourage learning and feedback loops**
  Encouraging employees to participate in impact measurement can help sustain commitment to ESG objectives. SMEs can implement feedback mechanisms, such as monthly team reviews of ESG progress, allowing teams to adjust and improve activities based on results.

- **Start with small wins**
  SMEs can foster a culture of measurement by starting with achievable goals that build confidence and show quick results. For instance, reducing office energy use or implementing a recycling program demonstrates the benefits of measurement and creates a foundation for larger ESG initiatives.

Conclusion

For SMEs, measuring ESG impact doesn't require extensive resources or complex systems. By establishing clear objectives, selecting relevant metrics, and using a structured impact measurement framework, SMEs can effectively track and communicate their ESG progress. This adaptable framework, originally developed for modern slavery initiatives, offers a valuable tool for SMEs aiming to make a positive impact across a range of ESG areas, ultimately contributing to sustainable and resilient business growth.

Chapter 7
The Business Case for ESG

Key Drivers to Doing Good in Business

A Melbourne-based apparel and merchandise company, Merchgirls, has had a long-standing commitment to reducing their impact on the environment. It used to be that when someone made a purchase, the retail assistant would wrap the item in tissue, put a sticker on the package, and then put it into a glossy bag with ribbon handles. While it might not be apparent immediately, all these packaging items are, in fact, based on single-use plastics—yes, even the tissue paper— and are not at all recyclable. The other side of their inventory management meant that stock arriving is packed overseas in heavy plastic wrapping and Styrofoam.[42]

In 2015, the company looked at what they could and could not control (i.e., what they sent out as well as what they received) and boldly decided to go cold turkey on all single-use plastics (SUP).

They now work face to face with their suppliers to talk about their business commitments and help them see the value in wrapping their goods in sustainable ways. They have also advised that any SUP will be promptly returned. On top of this, the company has a commitment to using safe dyes and recycled paper in their locally made stationery products. They also offset their greenhouse gas emissions in transport by planting trees through local initiatives in Australia. It's through this company's commitment to researching and implementing sustainable solutions that the company has positioned itself as a market leader and influencer in the merchandise sector and opened the door to business with large corporations and government entities who have a commitment to partner with small businesses who set clear standards on environmental and social practices.

We could go on to show how they are smashing other ESG goals, but the point to make in this chapter is what is driving their "green" behaviour and what might drive yours. So, what drives you to make a positive impact on people and planet? Are you going to embrace ESG just because you have to, because you feel it's "the right thig to do", or because it will improve your business's performance and profitability? When it comes to integrating ESG into your business DNA, there are at least three main drivers at play:

- Ethical
- Legal
- Commercial

What do we mean by Ethical, Legal and Commercial?
The Ethical Imperative

Although we all use a moral lens to approach life, our ethics vary. They could stem from a religious or spiritual conviction, either actively expressed or more of a legacy (cultural trait) passed down through the family and community history. They could also come from a more secular worldview based on enlightenment ideals (learned and assumed), or a combination of influences.

It's probably safe to say that most people want to be treated the same way you do, with clean air, soil, and water to live and work in. That's the ethical driver—a spectrum of private impulses embedded in culture that drive behaviour and the true source of the "why".

The Legal Mandate

In addition to ethics, many business owners are driven by what is legal and regulated by governments at all levels. When it comes to law, all businesses in Australia are governed at a minimum by the Corporations Act 2001 and by other regulatory bodies like Fair Work, ATO, and ASIC. Other standards and guidelines direct business behaviour with state-based nuances. In the world of ESG, the legal case may be a question of either regulatory compliance or alignment (if there is no reporting directive to be applied). Thus, if a business is only interested in their legal obligations, they will ask the question "In isolation, the legal case leads to a question of mandatory minimums: What is the minimum I must do to comply with the law and accepted regulations?"

The Commercial Value

When it comes to commerce, you wouldn't be in business if you weren't driven by the desire for financial gain and the commercial value of your products or services. In the world of ESG, perhaps you'll be driven by the commercial value of your ESG investments—investing in ESG impact areas, where your return on an investment in doing good is based on access to new business, markets, capital investment, and even tax incentives. NYU Stern (2021) examined 1,000+ studies (a meta-analysis) on the financial impact of companies adopting ESG measures. Fifty-eight per cent of studies found that ESG actions had a positive impact on financial performance; only 8% found that ESG had a negative financial effect.[43] A long-term study by the Harvard Business School found that "high sustainability" companies significantly outperformed low-ESG peers in stock returns and Return on Assets (ROI) over an 18-year period.[44]

The apparel and merchandise company mentioned above is driven primarily by its own ethical desire to do good by people and the planet. It That is what drives its business purpose and strategy, and year by year the owners are finding new ways to do better. It is through this lens that they commit to business solutions that create commercial value in the long term, and they see this as adding tremendous brand value to their business. This is measured through their own ESG impact framework through which they clearly articulate the problem they are looking to solve, their current and future solutions, and the impact made outside the business. In addition, they track what business is won and the criteria set for tendering that includes key areas of social and environmental sustainability. So, in addition to finding ways to do good, they are also guided by aligning their business practices with what their corporate and government clients are mandated to do.

Exploring the ESG Business Case

Doing good for people and planet comes at a cost… a cost that is worth it!

Regardless of any cost associated with doing good for people and planet, you will need to make your own personal and your own business decisions about the value of doing so. And we urge you to consider this based on the evidence we're presenting as to why it's of value.

In today's market landscape, small business owners face increasing pressure from consumers, investors, and regulatory bodies to adopt business practices that are good for both people and planet. This is despite some of the pushback we described in Chapter 2. We propose that integrating ESG is the new normal. Evidence suggests that integrating ESG into business practices—regardless of industry or location—can drive significant financial performance and enhance brand value, like the apparel and merchandise company described above.

Let's explore the main features of the business case for integrating ESG into your business DNA. (Note that what we are describing here reflects market trends over the past few years. As the integration of ESG into business strategy evolves, so will the business case. Some levers will take priority over others and new levers may emerge.)

Attracting Investment and Finance

First and foremost, companies that integrate ESG are better positioned to attract capital investment. According to recent reports, funds that prioritise ESG have shown resilience during economic downturns and greater overall returns.[45] In 2022, Global ESG Monitor noted that major banks in Australia and Europe are embedding ESG scoring into SME credit assessments.[46]

For small businesses, aligning with ESG standards can open doors to new funding opportunities, as more venture capital and private equity firms prioritise sustainable portfolios.47 Between 2021 and 2024, the growth of sustainable investment in Australia accelerated. According to the Responsible Investment Association Australasia (RIAA) and other financial institutions, capital investment in sustainable ventures grew by an estimated 20%–25% annually during this period.48 By the end of 2023, responsible investment assets accounted for nearly 50% of the total assets under management in Australia, surpassing the $2 trillion mark. This influx of investment not only fuels growth but also contributes to a company's long-term stability.

In a landmark 2017 study, the Boston Consulting Group (BCG) introduced the concept of Total Societal Impact (TSI), defined as the total benefit a company delivers to society through its core business. Importantly, BCG demonstrated a direct and statistically significant link between strong ESG performance and business value in terms of both market valuation and profit margins. Across five major industries, BCG found that companies that were top performers in specific ESG topics (such as environmental footprint or equal opportunity) enjoyed valuation multiples 3%–19% higher than median performers, all else being equal. These ESG leaders also had profit margins up to 12.4 percentage points higher than industry peers.[49]

While the study focused on large firms, the implications for SMEs are clear: targeted ESG improvements, especially those that align with core business capabilities, can yield not just social impact but substantial financial gain. Investors and lenders increasingly favour companies with strong ESG credentials, and this includes small business ventures and startups.

Attracting and Retaining Business

By integrating ESG into their business strategy, small businesses can open the door to new business including achieving preferred supplier status with government agencies and large corporations, retaining business, and forming joint ventures. We see this through the rise in business opportunities that are made available for small businesses that are certified as "Social Enterprises" by Social Traders. According to their 2024 Impact Report, "businesses have spent $1.1 billion with certified social enterprises over the last seven years", and "social procurement spend with certified social enterprises also hit an all-time high of $257 million. Sixty-two per cent of business members increased their spend in the past year, which meant that 80% of certified social enterprises increased their trading revenue."[50]

In the Australian market at least, having the right governance and risk management frameworks in place is strategic for attracting business (as discussed in Chapter 4). By governance, we refer to having key policies in place, a portfolio of policies that act as "controls" on certain business functions and processes. Some policies might also have a corresponding mechanism in place, like a grievance mechanism. By risk management, we refer to having a clear understanding of all the risks to your business as well as knowing what risks you might present for another company that you are looking to do business with. In relation to ESG, this means understanding risks like forced labour and child labour in the supply of goods and services, as we've discussed earlier.

Eighty per cent of large corporate buyers now screen suppliers for ESG performance. (RIAA, 2024)

By stepping up to the business goals of other businesses, they are opening the door to new business. A 2024 RIAA survey found 80% of large corporate buyers now screen suppliers for ESG performance; 63% require SMEs to submit basic ESG disclosures.[51] Under the Australian Government's Sustainable Procurement Guidelines, agencies must assess ESG credentials in supplier evaluations, including modern slavery, emissions, and social responsibility.[52] So, for small and medium-sized enterprises (SMEs), ESG adoption is more than a moral decision—it's a strategic one. From cutting costs and managing risks to winning tenders and attracting talent, ESG integration drives tangible business value. A growing body of global and Australian research confirms this.

Let's examine the Return On Investment of ESG investments and demonstrate how businesses can balance initial costs with long-term benefits. Case studies from Australian companies illustrate how embracing ESG can lead to competitive advantage and greater profitability.

Mitigating Risk

This leads to the question of risk mitigation. As raised in Chapter 4, companies that align with ESG standards are more adept at identifying and addressing potential risks, whether they are related to environmental disruptions, social conflicts, or governance failures.[53] For instance, businesses with transparent supply chains are less likely to be affected by sudden regulatory changes or public backlash that could otherwise disrupt operations and damage reputation. A KPMG Global ESG Survey (2023) found ESG-mature SMEs had faster recovery rates from climate events and supply chain shocks.[54] Everfocus noted that Queensland SMEs with documented ESG policies were three times more likely to have disaster insurance, business continuity plans, and robust supplier diversification .[55]

Brand Reputation

By integrating ESG into their business strategy, small businesses can enhance their brand reputation. Increasingly, consumers are being driven by values, by brands that can clearly demonstrate how they are benefiting people and planet. They are attracted by disrupters in the market, the outlier who bucks the status quo, often in controversial or "cheeky" ways. Consider the impact that *Tony's Chocolonely* is making to improve the lives of cocoa farmers and their families while calling the shots on what centuries-old chocolatiers are failing to do.[56] The company devotes a whole landing page with links to reports and blogs about the impact they are making, including how they work directly with 17,740 cocoa farmers in Ghana and Côte d'Ivoire and are committed to paying them a premium above market rates to ensure a living wage. What's interesting about the chocolatier is their high level of transparency, research, and reporting on how they work with both growers and retailers. Consider also *Who Gives a Crap* and how they tap into the mainstream Australian humour to point out the essential role of sanitation to aid global health targets while using recycled paper in their products.[57]

In addition, businesses that demonstrate a clear and measurable commitment to sustainability and social responsibility enjoy greater customer loyalty.[58] As many small businesses are business-to-consumer (B2C), this commitment can be a significant drawcard in terms of attracting local community support.[59] A strong ESG profile acts as a valuable differentiator in competitive markets and is a signal to individual consumers that the business is not just profit-driven but purpose-oriented.

Balancing the Costs and the Long-term Benefits

A common concern among small business owners is the initial cost of adopting ESG practices. Whether it's investing in energy-efficient equipment, implementing better labour standards, or improving supply chain transparency, the up-front costs (or investment) can seem daunting. However, the key to overcoming this hurdle is understanding the long-term benefits that outweigh the initial outlay.[60]

For example, transitioning to energy-efficient processes can significantly reduce utility bills over time. A small manufacturing business that installs solar panels or energy-saving machinery may face high initial costs, but within a few years, these investments typically pay for themselves through reduced operational expenses.[61]

Further, businesses that are proactive in adopting sustainable practices are less vulnerable to regulatory penalties and are better prepared for future compliance requirements. This forward-thinking approach reduces the risk of unexpected costs related to environmental and social governance legislation.[62]

It is important to add here that the long-term return on investment may be more social in nature and have a great economic benefit on a particular community rather than on you. Being able to apply this logic may demand some lateral thinking, but in time this will work to your advantage. At Unchained, as part of our social impact commitments with Social Traders and B-Corp, we reserve 5% of our revenue in order to make donations to the Freedom Business Alliance, who provide vocational training and meaningful employment to the survivors of modern slavery and human trafficking. We also give of our time and expertise pro bono to participate in not-for-profit advisory boards and committees. These commitments ensure that while we address the demand side of modern slavery, we are supporting grass roots initiatives that are working to address the supply side. Our commitment is commensurate with the size of our business, and as we scale, so will our impact.

Cost Reduction through Employee Engagement

The return on ESG investments can also be seen in employee retention and productivity. Small businesses that prioritise ESG often find that employees are more engaged and loyal, which leads to lower turnover rates and recruitment costs. This is especially important given that many small businesses compete for talent against larger companies. An attractive workplace culture, underpinned by strong ESG values, can be a decisive factor for job seekers.[63] According to Deloitte, ESG alignment is now a top consideration for job seekers, especially among young Australians.[64]

The importance of good business practices has risen sharply among younger employees in recent years. Multiple surveys and studies have shown that for Millennials and Generation Z, responsible corporate behaviour is a critical factor when choosing employers. For example, according to Deloitte and Cone Communications, over 75% of Millennials say they are willing to take a pay cut to work for a socially responsible company. For Gen Z, studies show that around 70%–80% of Gen Z employees view a company's environmental and social responsibility as a top priority in deciding where to work. Between 2020 and 2023, the importance placed on corporate responsibility by younger employees increased by an estimated 10%–15%.[65]

Key Steps for Small Business Owners

The arguments for embracing ESG principles in any business, especially a small to medium-sized company already concerned about compliance, risk management, growth strategies, and employee retention, is an evolving case study. To make this easier, here are some key steps you can take:

- **Start small, scale strategically:** Begin with manageable ESG initiatives that align with the business's current resources and current capacity. For instance, transitioning to eco-friendly packaging or sourcing local materials can be cost-effective starting points. Many regulatory bodies on packaging provide tools and educational resources to help with this.

- **Consider what is important to your customers:** If you are a business-to-business company, be familiar with what is important to them, so that you satisfy their tender process and contribute to their ESG goals. In our engagement with business, the key priorities include assessing Greenhouse Gas emissions (GHG), attending to the issue of human rights and modern slavery, and having a clear data/cybersecurity strategy.

- **Identify what areas of ESG you *are* committed to** in the short and long term, and what position statement you can make to guide your decision making.

- **Develop a practical policy portfolio:** Having clear policies that back up what you stand for (i.e., clean energy; human rights) is a good starting point. Policies do not have to be lengthy, but they need to be relevant, current, and easily understood and applied by everyone in the business. Note: to make policies relevant they must function as controls for the actual work you are doing to improve environmental, social or governance performance.[66]

- **Leverage your story for marketing:** An ESG initiative is not just an internal change but a compelling story to share with customers. As such, it's important to integrate what you are doing with your brand story, including websites, social media, and direct customer communications (e-newsletters, posters/flyers, and catalogues).

- **Invest in employee training:** Building awareness and commitment among employees ensures that ESG principles are integrated into your company culture. A well-trained team can implement sustainable practices more effectively. Consider what kind of awareness training everyone in the organisation can complete. Then consider what skills training is needed for those team members who are responsible for sourcing and purchasing goods and services, who manage risk and compliance, etc.

- **Monitor and measure impact:** Use key performance indicators (KPIs) to track the success of what you are investing in. The merchandise and apparel firm, for example, has a clear framework which covers the problems they are solving, their solution, and what result or outcome/benefit this contributes to. This kind of data will not only help fine-tune your strategy but also provide evidence to stakeholders of your company's ESG progress.

- And of course, be in contact with us! We offer services in strategy, analysis, training, policy development and reporting, as well as access to a hub of solution providers across the full range of ESG impact areas.

For small businesses, embedding ESG into their operations may seem a formidable challenge at first, but the potential rewards far outweigh the initial investments. From enhanced brand reputation and customer loyalty to financial gains and reduced risks, the business case for ESG is strong.[67] By balancing costs with long-term benefits and learning from the success stories of Australian companies, small business owners can create a road-map for sustainable growth. Embracing ESG is not just good for business; it is essential for remaining competitive and resilient in the modern market.

Chapter 8
Effective Stakeholder Engagement

Enabling, Training and Communication

The Australian-based arm of an international charity that supports impoverished people in developing countries made a firm commitment to addressing the risk of forced labour and child labour in the supply of merchandise that the organisation sells in order to support their work abroad. This organisation's commitment to addressing these human rights violations was voluntary and excelled beyond the compliance requirement of many listed companies that are mandated to comply with the Australian *Modern Slavery Act 2018 (Cth)*. One key feature of their commitment was how they engaged with their suppliers, many of them micro businesses scattered throughout India, Nepal, and Sri Lanka.

Acknowledging the challenges of self-assessment questionnaires to gain clarity on the steps that their suppliers were taking to identify and address the risk of workplace exploitation, the charity set up an online supplier workshop for all suppliers and asked Unchained Solutions to help guide the discussion. It was during this relational approach to due diligence that the suppliers gained a greater understanding of what the charity's questions on human rights meant and how they could support their client to address these issues in partnership with them. Since that meeting, this pool of suppliers have applied themselves to understanding more about possible forced labour risks among people who supply raw materials to them. They have also worked to put more of what they are doing in policy documents that will standardise their processes and help them engage other buyers in different countries.

This experience highlights the transformative potential of stakeholder engagement in achieving ESG objectives. For it is through intentional engagements with local communities, employees, or external experts, that small businesses can precisely align their operations with broader sustainability goals. In this chapter, we explore:

- How to identify and engage key stakeholders that enable your business to function

- How to understand their influence on ESG outcomes

- How to communicate effectively to build trust and loyalty

Rather than work through each stakeholder group, this chapter explores how SMEs can hold the space for others to be enabled, how they can provide awareness and skills training to increase capabilities and develop their team culture, and how they can communicate effectively with the market through weaving their impact into their branding, funding pitch, and position statements.

Identifying and Engaging Key Stakeholders

To be truly effective in making an impact on ESG, you need to consider where your business fits within the broader market eco-system and who the key stakeholders are within it that support your business. Knowing who is around you, who contributes to your business strategy, and who might benefit from the efforts you are making is a key criterion for making a lasting social and environmental impact. By doing so, you recognise that your best efforts are located within a broader ecosystem of good practices and that your business is a small, yet important, link in the chain.

We mentioned in Chapter 6 that being effective is not achieved simply through compliance or through risk avoidance. Making a lasting impact means looking for ways to benefit others and contribute to their success. As we consider the "engagement" component of ESG activities, we will focus on the role of people who are both internal and external to your business. We will also consider the impact measurement dimension, realising that all our work will involve the pursuit of positive outcomes (in terms of social benefit) and reduction of negative outcomes (in terms of risk mitigation).

Consider this list of stakeholders

- Local communities: remediating past harms and building up communities
- Employees
- Suppliers and distributers, transport, and logistics
- Consumers or corporate clients
- Investors, funders, and lenders*
- Business partnerships (referral networks, channel partners, and joint ventures)
- External experts

A way of describing this social ecosystem is your value chain.

As the role of investors, funders, and lenders was discussed in Chapter 7, they will not feature in this chapter.

Capacity building: Creating spaces for others to thrive

A key dynamic in stakeholder engagement is creating and holding spaces for other organisations to develop their own capacity to thrive and make an impact. This includes working with local communities and supplier networks and harnessing the collective energy from key business partners.

Local Communities: Partners in Social and Environmental Impact

Local communities are often the most visible external stakeholders, directly experiencing the impacts of a business's operations. Effective engagement with these communities is essential for addressing environmental and social concerns while building goodwill and exploring practical ways of improving their social and economic opportunities.

Local community engagement can be approached in two main ways. The first approach is taking positive action in response to past harms that your business may have either caused, contributed to, or had a direct impact on.[68] This remedy-based approach[69] may be difficult to discern (it often is for large corporations) with the impact on people being felt way beyond what is immediately visible. Doing something meaningful may also be out of your control. Your business is part of a larger business ecosystem in which you have a role to play, however small, in minimising harm to people through how your business operates locally and how the goods and services you buy are made and delivered. Further, the impact on a community of people may be indirect and focussed more on impact on a local environment that impacts the quality of life of the community who depend on it for their own survival. EcoPlast SA is a South African SME that shifted to circular economy practices by recycling plastic waste, engaging local communities in environmental education, and creating employment opportunities. This deliberate approach not only reduced regional pollution but also fostered economic and social well-being in the surrounding area.[70]

The second step in taking positive action is using the profits from your business to support an underserved community in a remote location. This is the approach taken by Unchained Solutions, who as part of their Social Traders Certification, give 50% of their profits to other social enterprises who work directly with the survivors of human trafficking. Other approaches may be more direct, such as providing employment pathways for neurodivergent people. One of Exceptional's key initiatives is the establishment of the Xceptional Academy, which provides tailored training programs and coaching to prepare neurodivergent candidates for roles in software testing, data analysis, and other technology-related fields. These programs are designed to remove barriers to employment by focusing on the candidates' abilities and providing support throughout the hiring process.71 As small businesses find ways to support people from diverse backgrounds, directly or indirectly, and engage through mutual respect and shared goals, their efforts can yield extraordinary outcomes.

Suppliers, Distributers, Transport, and Logistics: Shared Responsibility for ESG Goals

Suppliers and other stakeholders within the supply chain, including distributors, transportation firms, and logistics, are integral to implementing ESG strategies. The Melbourne-based merchandise and apparel company mentioned earlier, Merchgirls, shows how small businesses can lead suppliers toward more sustainable practices. As part of their due diligence with suppliers in places like China, Vietnam, and Indonesia, the directors make annual trips to meet with factory managers and micro-business owners. During these trips, they share with suppliers what their goals are in terms of reducing the use of single-use plastics (SUP) and discuss alternative ways of protecting goods for transportation.

Further, recognising their dependence on large shipping and transport firms, they offset the emissions generated by planting trees in different location projects throughout Australia. In short, their efforts go beyond compliance, fostering innovation and collaboration that benefits both parties. By setting clear standards and offering practical support, they are helping their suppliers to build their own capacity and become active contributors to ESG goals rather than passive participants.

Business partnerships: Building capacity through shared values

Another key stakeholder group includes business leaders who are aligned with your current priorities and who you can collaborate with to increase your impact among local communities. Stephen's company, Unchained Solutions, has been committed to forming genuine partnerships with organisations who are making an impact among local communities in many parts of the world, primarily South-East Asia. Through Stephen's work on the advisory board of the Freedom Business Alliance, Unchained has contributed to improving the way that member organisations conduct their business operations through the development of a Code of Excellence.[72]

Most of the members are social enterprises who operate to make both a profit through global markets through their commitment to employing people who have experienced human trafficking or who are at risk of being exploited. This approach to business requires an acute understanding of trauma-informed care usually associated with health professionals, allied health and not-for-profits. The development of this Code included widespread stakeholder engagement and planning but led to an effective tool that can readily be integrated into any businesses' organisational structure.

To foster shared-value partnerships, effective engagements need to be interactive. Hosting feedback sessions or co-creation workshops invites stakeholders to contribute to solutions, fostering ownership and long-term collaboration.

Capability Building: Providing awareness and skills training for long-term culture change and impact

A second area of effective stakeholder engagement is investing in capability building. Whereas capacity building focuses on developing the systems and structures of a group at, say, the organisational level, capability building focuses on the skills and behaviours of the individual. Within this section, we've identified two main stakeholders: employees whose professional skills will be instrumental in advancing a company's social and environmental impact, and external experts whose technical skills can both equip the team and assist in developing the right organisational culture for long-term impact.

Employees: Transforming teams through skills development and culture change

Your team are your greatest asset and are key to achieving a positive impact on people and planet. Given your range of impact areas and the scope of skills required, it is important to provide training to teams. This could include offering high-level awareness education to everyone on the team, and more deep-dive skills training for those who will be at the forefront of implementing sustainability policies and procedures.

As with local communities, your team could also be the context for making the most impact. Consider the work of Busy Ability, a Queensland-based employment service provider that offers tailored support to individuals with disabilities, injuries, or health conditions, assisting them in finding and maintaining meaningful employment. Their services include personalized career planning, resume assistance, interview preparation, and connections with inclusive employers. They also provide ongoing support to ensure long-term job retention.73 Consider also Hotel Etico in the NSW Blue Mountains and their range of employee pathway programs. It is Australia's first social enterprise hotel employing and training young adults with intellectual disabilities. Through its two-year program, participants gain hands-on experience across hotel operations while developing independent living skills through its on-site Academy of Independence. Graduates transition to award-wage jobs in mainstream hospitality, demonstrating how structured workplace training can create meaningful social impact.[74]

External Experts: Securing ESG Efforts

Getting help with your ESG strategy could be essential. While we have made every effort to simplify the complex nature of ESG, there will be times when you will need the assistance of technical specialists who can help you achieve your long-term goals and ward off greenwashing accusations. For instance, under the environmental dimension, a lot of resources are available on good practice in recycling, sustainable packaging, and renewable energy, such as Cumberland Recycling Distribution Centre's Initiative[75] and Lactams, which developed an innovative biodegradable packaging solution using milk protein (casein).[76]

However, technical expertise may be required to help in calculating greenhouse gas emissions, redeploying energy and material outputs in new products (circular economy), and designing an emergency plan to mitigate environmental harm. Within governance, you may need expert advice on developing policies, implementing a grievance mechanism, and running a cybersecurity audit.

External experts may also be required to provide training on how to manage processes internally and measure the impact.

Going further, expertise may come in the form of certification bodies, industry associations, and partner organisations who can help you verify your progress. This was certainly the case for Unchained Solutions, who first achieved B-Corp certification in 2023. As a facilitation and advisory firm providing support to companies on their governance and risk management frameworks, it was critical that they had the same standards and controls in place. The intense level of scrutiny, accountability, and proof needed to show how they measure impact and plan to improve their score at the three-year renewal mark was a way for them to demonstrate their own commitment to good business practices, so that they could advise others with integrity.

Brand Integration: Effective communication to align with market expectations among consumers and corporate clients

A third dimension of stakeholder engagement relates to how an organisation communicates all the good work that they are doing to the broader market, thus appealing to the expectations of both individual consumers and corporate clients. Taylor & Grace is a Melbourne-based branding company that helps a lot of small businesses and charities to meaningfully show their ESG commitments through their brand narrative to build trust and strengthen their engagement with stakeholders. They warn their clients about "greenhushing"—the tendency to downplay a company's sustainability efforts for fear of criticism. This can lead to missed opportunities to connect with audiences who want to see their authenticity and purpose.[77]

Having an effective strategy to communicate your efforts to make an impact on people and planet requires working out how to best share the different activities you are doing within the context of statements about your company's purpose and what you are looking to achieve.

The challenge is to communicate what you are actually doing, not just what you aspire to do or be, which can easily lead to things like greenwashing accusations and reputational damage.

Being able to communicate what you are doing is often overlooked. For instance, many small businesses are doing great things but neglect to have everything recorded in writing. The urgency of business survival and the priorities of making a sale often overshadow the not-so-urgent work of developing training packs, position statements, and policies. Moreover, these good activities may not be well integrated into websites and social media posts.

Modern consumer expectations:

As raised in Chapter 7, modern consumers, particularly Millennials and Gen Z, actively seek brands that reflect their values. According to the 2022 McCrindle Report, *Communicating Your Social Impact*, "More than nine in ten Gen Ys (93%) are more likely to engage with an organisation that clearly communicates its social impact compared to 80% of Baby Boomers. Social proofing is also more likely to occur, with younger Australians more likely to tell others about an organisation that clearly communicates its social impact (90% Gen Y cf. 86% Gen Z, 85% Gen X, 77% Baby Boomers).[78]

Plate It Forward is a NSW-based social enterprise that operates restaurants like Colombo Social and Kabul Social to support refugees, asylum seekers, and disadvantaged communities. Each meal purchased funds a meal for someone in need, and the enterprise provides employment and training to marginalised individuals. Since 2020, it has donated over 625,000 meals, created 169,000+ training hours, and paid $5 million in wages. By clearly communicating these outcomes, Plate It Forward strengthens customer trust and brand loyalty—particularly among Gen Y and Z consumers who value social proof and ethical business practices.[79]

Stakeholders connect with narratives that reflect genuine impact. The Melbourne-based apparel and merchandise manufacturer, Merchgirls, integrated its Single-Use Plastics (SUP) reduction journey into its brand story, sharing metrics and success stories through newsletters and social media. This built consumer trust and positioned the company as a leader in sustainable practices.[80]

Alignment with corporate clients and government agencies:

In a business-to-business (B2B) context, where the small business is often a supplier or service provider to a larger entity, branded position statements, policies, and certifications (i.e. an International Standard (ISO)) are key. For example, many large organisations, including corporations and government entities, require their suppliers to have robust policies, including a purpose statement. The "Big Three" policies these large organisations will look for are:

- Environment – energy use, resource management and environmental impact

- Health and Safety – how you will protect the health and safety of your employees and all those who work with you

- Quality – how you will design, create, and deliver the products and services that customers want, to the correct quality, at the correct time.

We can probably increase this to "The Big Four" now, and add Cyber-security to the list.

Different stakeholders require unique approaches. For example, while investors value data-driven insights, local communities prefer stories of tangible benefits. A dual strategy ensures messages resonate with all audiences.

A clear position statement on what you stand for in relation to human rights, diversity, and energy output is not something to keep hidden in a file. It is something to weave into your brand story. This, together with your impact measurement framework, becomes the means for communicating what you stand for, the steps you are taking to abide by that, and the steps you are taking to measure your progress—including all the road bumps along the way. (Making a positive impact will never be a linear process or a clean progression from A to B.)

One particularly powerful tool for embedding and communicating organisational values is a *Culture Book*. A Culture Book captures the essence of who you are as an organisation—your mission, vision, values, behaviours, rituals, and stories that bring your culture to life. It helps current and future team members understand not only what you do, but how and why you do it.

At 4T Consultants, our Culture Book is more than a document; it's a living reflection of the principles that guide our actions, from our commitment to good science, to how we celebrate success, support one another, and uphold integrity and sustainability in everything we do. Creating your own Culture Book doesn't need to be overwhelming. Start by gathering your founding story, core values, and the beliefs that underpin your daily decisions. Add in team rituals, quotes, and examples of behaviours you want to reinforce. Design it in your company's tone and style—whether formal or informal, digital or printed—so it genuinely reflects your identity. Used well, a Culture Book becomes a shared reference point, an onboarding tool, and a unifying force that strengthens engagement and trust across all stakeholders.

Like all change management processes, there will be trials and errors, experiments, and failures (from which you can fail-forward). A squeaky-clean communications strategy on ESG will be viewed as disingenuous. Your ESG story, much like your own personal story, needs to be nuanced to reflect a colourful experience.

Stakeholder engagement is fundamental to embedding ESG into a business. Through authentic partnerships with communities, suppliers, and employees, small businesses not only achieve compliance but also drive meaningful change. Whether it's collaborating with local villagers to create sustainable solutions or partnering with experts to ensure supply chain integrity, stakeholder engagement transforms challenges into opportunities for innovation and trust-building.

For small businesses, the journey to sustainability begins with meaningful conversations. By prioritising stakeholder engagement, these businesses are not only poised for resilience and growth but also set to lead a more sustainable future.

Chapter 9
Integrating ESG into Business Strategy

Integrating ESG into Your Business Strategy

Proskill Workwear Australia is a Melbourne-based small business that distributes sustainable safety wear licensed from Mascot Workwear in Denmark. Proskill's approach to ESG lies principally in their commitment to providing long-life products. demonstrating the achievement of significant financial and environmental savings including water, Co2 & landfill with countless companies and organisations achieving this. In addition, Mascot Workwear also ensures that people working in its factories operate under safe working conditions, with fair pay and the protection of human rights. Mascot's factories in Vietnam and Laos are SA8000 certified, meaning that they are subject to social compliance audits to ensure the protection of human rights for all workers.[81] Proskill clearly sees the value in making a positive impact on people and planet while leveraging their brand alignment with corporate clients.

In Chapter 7 we covered the business case for integrating ESG into your business strategy and operations. In this chapter, we consider the investment that you might need to make to realise your long-term ESG goals and preferred future and to make it part of your core operations For many small businesses, alignment with ESG standards, directives, and targets will mean short-term pain in terms of fixed costs (social compliance or security audits, system upgrades etc.), and variable costs (time and materials) to change the organisation's capacity and capabilities. The long-term gain, measured over time, is in business opportunities and competitiveness. However, it is also measured in non-financial ways, such as improvements to people's lives and livelihood, and improvements to the natural environment that underpins social and economic activity. If companies report only on their financial results, we shouldn't be surprised if that is what everyone else concentrates on. What gets monitored gets managed.

There are several possible investment areas to consider. This is not an exhaustive list, but it highlights the main ones that relate mostly to small business:

- Investment in executive-level meetings to monitor and report on ESG activities
- Investment in marketing strategies to benchmark the company's progress and to identify current and future trends
- Investment in your people to meet KPIs including encouraging personal goals
- Investment in supplier ESG credential screening for responsible sourcing and onboarding
- Investment in your own company's ESG credentials and attributes including certifications, audits, sustainable tech, and business solutions
- Investment in sustainable product development, packaging alternatives, and delivery options.

Investment in executive-level meetings to monitor and report on ESG activities

Time is one of the most significant investments a business owner can make. Effective ESG integration begins with ensuring ESG activities become a permanent fixture on the agenda for your regular management or team meetings. To fully embed ESG into your company, ensure you extend beyond traditional financial performance reviews to include discussions that encompass your ESG activities.

Key Components of ESG Monitoring and Reporting

- **Progress tracking**: Establish a system to monitor ESG initiatives, such as carbon reduction or community engagement, and provide detailed progress reports. Chapter 6 covered how you can start setting your company's goals and progress measures.

- **Cross-functional representation**: Include representatives from finance, operations, marketing, and human resources to ensure holistic integration of ESG across departments.

- **Technology tools:** Consider making use of ESG reporting software to track compliance. These tools allow you to streamline the measurement of KPIs, such as energy efficiency, supply chain transparency, or diversity metrics. Unchained offers an **Automated ESG Reporting Platform** powered by Trace Supply Chains Intelligence.

This platform is grounded in globally recognised frameworks and developed in collaboration with 70 global banks, trade organisations, and industry associations to provide a trusted source of information on supply certifications, accreditations and alignment with UN SDGs. It simplifies complex data analysis, offering clear and reliable insights that businesses can trust. This level of transparency and precision has been invaluable for our clients who are working to strengthen their ESG performance and credibility with corporate client and government entities.

Regular reviews create accountability, provide early identification of challenges, and ensure that ESG efforts align with broader business goals. While this requires an initial time investment, the long-term benefits of formally monitoring and reporting on ESG activities will outweigh the costs. The investment in time and personnel will ensure your investment dollars are working hard towards sustainable solutions.

Investment in marketing strategies to benchmark your company's progress and identify current and future trends

A well-thought-out marketing strategy is instrumental in communicating your ESG achievements to customers and stakeholders. In Chapter 8, we considered the importance of showcasing ESG as a core part of your brand identity and narrative to attract conscious consumers, investors, and business partners. Here, we focus more on two marketing strategies that will inform your business strategy with ESG activities.

- Conduct **market research** to understand customer priorities concerning sustainability and social responsibility. This provides clarity on the ESG areas that resonate most with your target audience. This could be conducted cheaply and inhouse through customer reviews, where customers are invited to share their preferences on certain ESG impact areas. A bigger investment would involve market research companies.

- Perform a **competitor analysis** to benchmark your progress and identify gaps in the market. For example, evaluate whether competitors have adopted green certifications, supply chain transparency tools, or circular economy practices. One of the easiest ways to do this is through an ESG AI-powered, cloud-based interface that draws on real-time international trade data and what certifications, accreditations, and memberships your competitors hold.

Investment in your people to meet KPIs including encouraging personal goals

Your employees are your most valuable asset in driving ESG initiatives. Aligning your human resources strategy with ESG goals ensures that your workforce is motivated, capable, and aligned with your mission. Culture is critical. Culture is where ESG comes to life—through daily actions, not just policies.

In Chapter 8, we covered the need to invest in ESG-specific training programs that equip your team with the knowledge to implement impactful strategies. Employees need to understand concepts like sustainability, carbon neutrality, and ethical supply chains to effectively integrate these into their daily responsibilities, both at a high (awareness) level and at a skills level.

Such capability training, though, needs to be matched with an investment in systems that measure their performance. This may include encouraging all team members to develop their own personal sustainability goals outside of work, which is a requirement of the B-Corp certification assessment tool.[82]

Here are some ways to integrate ESG goals into individual and team KPIs:

- Introduce a plan for reducing departmental energy consumption by a specific percentage every year.

- Allow your employees to volunteer their time on projects that benefit underserved local communities.

- Plan to diversify your supplier base to incorporate female-owned businesses and Indigenous businesses. Set a target on increasing this by percentage base over a two- to three-year period.

These KPIs should connect with your overall organisational ESG objectives. For example, an employee responsible for sourcing and onboarding suppliers could have a KPI tied to engaging suppliers that meet specific sustainability criteria.

Another strategy for your team encouraged by the B-Corp framework is to align your company's values with your team's personal goals. Team members could agree to make changes to what they buy for their own use. They become conscious consumers who buy only sustainably made products that are free from child labour and forced labour risks, and are locally sourced to reduce carbon emissions. They could also be encouraged to review their transport habits, water usage, and recycling. By encouraging employees to set and achieve family or personal sustainability goals, such as waste reduction or community involvement, your business can create a culture of shared responsibility and purpose.

Investment in supplier ESG credential screening for responsible sourcing and onboarding

The suppliers you choose directly impact your ESG performance. Suppliers can help you reduce your dependence on single-use plastics, enhance your commitment to workplace health and safety, and be part of your overall cybersecurity strategy. For this to occur, you first need to understand who your company buys from and what work they are doing to make a positive impact on people and planet.

In our discussion on monitoring and reporting, and then in marketing, we talked about how AI- technology can be leveraged to track your company's progress and assess the status of your competitors. It can also be used to improve transparency and accountability in your supply chain. Consider the following strategies:

Supplier Screening and Onboarding

Screening suppliers for ESG compliance is crucial. Tools such as Unchained's Automated ESG Reporting Platform powered by Trace Supply Chain Intelligence offer AI-driven and trade data technology that can:

- assess a supplier's sustainability credentials
- track their compliance with ethical and sustainable practices in relation to the UN Sustainable Development Goals (SDGs)
- identify risks such as forced labour or environmental violations

Pre-qualification ensures that only ESG-aligned suppliers are onboarded, reducing reputational and operational risks.

Building Long-Term Relationships

Investing in long-term partnerships with ethical suppliers can drive mutual growth. Offer training sessions or share resources to help suppliers meet your ESG standards. This collaborative approach enhances trust and creates shared value.

Showcasing Success

Highlighting your work with ethical suppliers can enhance your brand's ESG narrative. Share case studies or co-branded initiatives that show your commitment to sustainable partnerships.

Investment in ESG credentials and attributes including certifications, audits, sustainable tech and business solutions

Certifications and frameworks validate your ESG commitment and signal to stakeholders that you're serious about sustainability. The right credentials can open doors to new markets, partnerships, and opportunities. Consider the following certifications, accreditations, and memberships:

ISO, SA, and Risk Management Frameworks

ISO Certifications:

- 9001 (Quality management)

- ISOISO 14001 (Environmental management)

- ISO 45001 (Occupational health and safety management) demonstrates compliance with global ESG standards.

- ISO 20400 Sustainable Procurement offers guidance on how to ensure the goods you purchase are good for people and planet.

- ISO 2700 Information security, cybersecurity and privacy protection

- **SA8000**: This certification, focused on social accountability, ensures ethical treatment of workers in your supply chain.

Certifications:

- B-Corp

- Social Traders

- WeConnect

Memberships and Social Compliance Audits:

- SEDEX SMETA

- ETI

- BSCI

Cybersecurity and Data Protection

ESG extends beyond the environment to include robust governance practices. Conduct cybersecurity audits and invest in system optimization to protect sensitive data. A failure in this area can undermine stakeholder trust and disrupt operations.

Switching to Sustainable Banking and Energy

Partner with financial institutions and energy providers that align with your ESG values. Sustainable banking options, for example, invest in green projects and exclude industries such as fossil fuels or arms manufacturing.

Investment in Sustainable Product Development, packaging alternatives, and delivery options

Product development is a key avenue for ESG integration, particularly for businesses in manufacturing, retail, or logistics. Whether it's through sustainable materials or inclusive hiring practices, innovation aligned with ESG principles can drive growth while benefiting the environment and society.

Upcycling and Circular Economy Processes

For manufacturers, upcycling waste materials into new products minimizes waste and reduces costs. Incorporating circular economy practices—such as carbon capture or water recycling—can further improve resource efficiency and environmental impact.

Sustainable Packaging Alternatives

Eliminating single-use plastics is not only an environmental necessity but also an opportunity to appeal to conscious consumers. Explore alternatives like biodegradable, recyclable, or reusable packaging materials. You may wish to review the 5 Rs of waste management from Chapter 1.

Offsetting Emissions in Logistics

Partner with logistics providers who offset carbon emissions through initiatives like reforestation or investing in renewable energy. This demonstrates your commitment to reducing your supply chain's carbon footprint.

Creating Employment Pathways

Incorporate social responsibility into product development by creating employment opportunities for underserved communities. For example, hiring neurodivergent individuals or offering apprenticeships to disadvantaged youth not only builds social equity but also enriches your organizational culture.

Conclusion

Integrating ESG into your business strategy requires a multi-faceted approach, balancing investments in time, people, processes, and innovation. For small businesses, the journey may seem daunting, but the rewards are well worth the effort. By committing to ESG principles, you will position your company as a leader in your industry, capable of driving sustainable growth and making a lasting impact on the world. Remember, ESG integration is a continuous process. As markets evolve, so must your strategies.

We encourage you to stay proactive, embrace innovation, and ensure that your values remain at the core of every decision you make. Your efforts to make a positive and lasting impact on people and planet through your business has the potential to do more than you realise when you stick to your convictions, collaborate with others, and inspire the next generation of change makers.

Your Fast-Track

to ESG Readiness

There is always so much to do to become fully ESG ready. But it doesn't have to be a hard slog with new teams and endless discussions. You could easily put in place much of what has been discussed here by contacting **Unchained Solutions** and working through some simple strategy options with Stephen and the team there.

Start with a visit to (*www.unchainedsolutions.com.au/book*) and download an easy to follow checklist. While you're there, check out some of the many resources available for businesses like yours, wanting to increase your impact on the planet and those you do business with, and those your business serves.

Acknowledgements

To the small and medium business leaders who show tremendous courage in making a positive impact on people and planet.

This book would not have been possible except for the contribution of a few people who assisted me in creating time for writing, gathering insights and research, and then bringing my words to life. I'm especially wish to thank the Unchained team for their case study research, insights and feedback, for our business partners who are part of our solution hub, and to my small business clients who demonstrate good business practices.

In particular, I would like to thank my co-author Bronwyn for helping me jump start this project and writing, for sharing, and exploring it with me as we pulled it together under the guiding hand of Dixie, Rosemary and Ammie at Indie Experts, our excellent and well-humoured publishing team.

Most of all I wish to thank my wife and business partner, Sarah, for creating the space for me to publish. Thank you for your patience, your encouragement, and your uncanny ability to stay calm when I most definitely wasn't. I'm not sure whether you deserve a medal or a holiday, but you've certainly earned both.

Stephen

Plan Smarter. Act Bolder.

Make a lasting difference.

When it comes to planning and executing ESG policies and managing the risks and relationships you have with stakeholders in your business, it's about more than just a quick conversation with your team. Real planning is critical to getting this right, and helpful resources and experience to navigate your way forward is what you get with **Bronwyn Reid**. Starting with an **UP Session** to Unpack and Prioritise what you have, what you need, and how best to proceed forward.

A multi-award winning business person and thought leader, holding your hand through this process is on offer starting with a conversation.

Please visit *www.bronwynreid.com.au/ESGBook* for more details and bonus resources.

Start with a visit to (*www.unchainedsolutions.com.au/book*) and download an easy to follow checklist. While you're there, check out some of the many resources available for businesses like yours, wanting to increase your impact on the planet and those you do business with, and those your business serves.

Acknowledgements

To the small and medium business owners and managers who show up every day with integrity, care, and purpose - thank you.

You might not have realised you were "doing ESG," but if you've ever paid a supplier on time, hired someone who needed a chance, looked after your people, supported your community, or done something to minimise your environmental impact, you're already part of the movement. Thank you for proving that success and ethics go hand in hand, even without a consultant (or an acronym) telling you so. You are quietly making the world better, one decision at a time.

To Ian (my husband, business partner, and the man who has now survived three rounds of "just one more edit…"), thank you for your patience, your encouragement, and your uncanny ability to stay calm when I most definitely wasn't. I'm not sure whether you deserve a medal or a holiday, but you've certainly earned both.

And to Dixie, my publisher, steady guide, and book shepherd, thank you for once again nursing me through the book-writing process with a perfect mix of insight, humour, and well-timed nudges. I suspect you knew I'd write a third before I did. You were right.

For my husband and business partner, Ian. Thank you for getting me through a third book.

Bronwyn

About the Authors

Dr Stephen Morse is the CEO of Unchained Solutions Pty Ltd, a Sydney-based social enterprise and certified B-Corp that enables organisations to make a meaningful contribution to the UN Sustainable Development Goals and improve their ESG reporting and CSR commitments. Stephen has over 25 years' experience in entrepreneurial leadership in the not-for-profit and private sectors, both in Australia and overseas. He's a seasoned public speaker, thought leader, author and strategist who brings an engaging and refreshing perspective on how industry professionals and business owners can make a positive and lasting impact on people and planet. Stephen obtained his Doctorate in Human Trafficking Intervention through Fuller Theological Seminary in 2016, and MBA through University of Technology Sydney in 2020. He currently serves on the Advisory Board of the Freedom Business Alliance and chairs the Ethics Committee of the Australasian Supply Chain Institute.

Bronwyn Reid is a business owner, author, and unapologetic advocate for small and medium enterprises (SMEs). With nearly three decades of experience running her own award-winning environmental consultancy in regional Australia, Bronwyn understands both the challenges and the triumphs of life in small business. She has made it her mission to help SMEs punch above their weight, particularly when it comes to navigating supply chains, big-company procurement, and the sometimes-bewildering world of sustainability and ESG.

This is Bronwyn's third book, and she still hasn't learned how to write one without coffee, deadline panic, or her husband Ian reminding her that sleep is useful. She is also a sought-after speaker and mentor, passionate about regional development, ethical business, and reminding the world that small companies can do big things. And often do.